Free Listening

SERIES EDITORS *Marco Abel and Roland Végső*

PROV
OCAT
IONS

Something in the world forces us to think.
—Gilles Deleuze

The world provokes thought. Thinking is nothing but the human response to this provocation. Thus, the very nature of thought is to be the product of a provocation. This is why a genuine act of provocation cannot be the empty rhetorical gesture of the contrarian. It must be an experimental response to the historical necessity to act. Unlike the contrarian, we refuse to reduce provocation to a passive noun or a state of being. We believe that real moments of provocation are constituted by a series of actions that are best defined by verbs or even infinitives—verbs in a modality of potentiality, of the promise of action. To provoke is to intervene in the present by invoking an as yet undecided future radically different from what is declared to be possible in the present and, in so doing, to arouse the desire for bringing about change. By publishing short books from multiple disciplinary perspectives that are closer to the genres of the manifesto, the polemical essay, the intervention, and the pamphlet than to traditional scholarly monographs, "Provocations" hopes to serve as a forum for the kind of theoretical experimentation that we consider to be the very essence of thought.

www.provocationsbooks.com

Free Listening

NAOMI WALTHAM-SMITH

UNIVERSITY OF NEBRASKA PRESS · LINCOLN

The University of Nebraska Press is part
of a land-grant institution with campuses
and programs on the past, present, and
future homelands of the Pawnee, Ponca,
Otoe-Missouria, Omaha, Dakota, Lakota,
Kaw, Cheyenne, and Arapaho Peoples,
as well as those of the relocated Ho-
Chunk, Sac and Fox, and Iowa Peoples.

∞

Library of Congress Cataloging-
in-Publication Data
Names: Waltham-Smith, Naomi, 1983– author.
Title: Free listening / Naomi Waltham-Smith.
Description: Lincoln: University of
Nebraska Press, [2024] | Series: Provocations
| Includes bibliographical references.
Identifiers: LCCN 2024022981
ISBN 9781496234520 (paperback;
acid-free paper)
ISBN 9781496242167 (epub)
ISBN 9781496242174 (pdf)
Subjects: LCSH: Progressivism (United
States politics) | Listening—Political
aspects. | Freedom of expression—United
States. | BISAC: PHILOSOPHY / Political |
POLITICAL SCIENCE / Political Freedom
Classification: LCC JK2316 .W365 2024 |
DDC 303.48/40973—dc23/eng/20240722
LC record available at
https://lccn.loc.gov/2024022981

Set in OFL Sorts Mill Goudy by K. Andresen.
Designed by N. Putens.

CONTENTS

PROVOCATIONS

No Listening, No Peace!
On the one hand, this echo of the familiar demand "no justice, no peace" suggests that listening—if only the state were to make good on it—would bring about an end to protest and dissent to the extent that a democratic demand would have been met. On the other hand, however, the reworked slogan points to a less encouraging idea: as (staged) performance, listening is actually designed to bring about an end to dissenting speech insofar as it seeks to subdue it through a false rhetorical promise or, to borrow the late Lauren Berlant's term, a cruel optimism. The alternatives mean that listening is the very condition of (im)possibility that underpins what is struggled over in debates about free speech. It is also what sustains, through an attachment to the feeling of being heard, an erroneous translation of audibility into expression. Free speech presupposes an equality of being heard when there is no such actually existing equality of audibility or any actually existing listening that would guarantee it. For there to be any such freedom would require the invention of new conditioned and conditional modalities of listening each and every time enacted in the name of the unconditional listening named in this demand.

Forget Free Speech, Fight for Free Listening!

It is a common refrain that the left needs to reclaim the mantle of free speech from the right. Somewhat provocatively, I argue that progressive forces should focus their efforts instead on what I am calling *free listening*—that is, the kind of listening that would make possible a more equal audibility, or at least a struggle for it. From this standpoint, it becomes possible to debunk reactionary claims to a monopoly on being "canceled" and instead expose how such campaigns in the name of free speech can be wielded further to silence marginalized voices—in other words, that freedom in the hands of the already powerful propagates, and is indeed premised upon, the unfreedom of the powerless. Insofar as speech, as performativity, is bound up with a capacity, power, or potentiality, it already "silences" the domain of aurality as the terrain of the noisy other, excluded from the rational, articulate *logos*. A focus on free listening aims to undercut this fundamentally colonialist understanding of freedom and democracy that condemns the racialized other, excluded from the sphere of human rationality, to always "speaking out of place," as the title of David Palumbo-Liu's recent book on activism has it.

Transparency Is Overrated, Defend Secrecy!

It is common for the liberal center to bemoan the evacuation of truth in contemporary politics, the rise of disinformation, and the spread of "fake news." In the first instance, such phenomena are not entirely new, although their conspicuousness and salience may have increased due to algorithmically driven propaganda and the reemergence of strongman leaders of right-nationalist vehicles. And yet, as Michel Foucault's late work illustrates, threats to truth-telling have been around since ancient Greece and may, in fact, be a condition of the political in general and democracy in particular. Coupled with appeals to "truth" are often demands for transparency in political life. It is difficult, though, to tease such values apart from increasingly authoritarian modes of surveillance and exposure, exacerbated by the COVID-19 pandemic. Against this liberal common sense, the book seeks to recover a value of secrecy, which is not without ambivalence, but whose treasure might usefully be pried away from the toxic suspicion and corrupt underbelly of modern power instead to shelter a reserve of freedom and anticolonial resistance. This idea draws upon critical traditions within psychoanalysis as practices of listening that, far from exposing the hidden unsaid, instead work to protect the regenerative resources of veiling and guarding within. Such "gentle listening," in the words of the late Anne Dufourmantelle, provides a template for care in a world increasingly ravaged by aural violence.

Abolition Democracy, Not Cancel Culture!

Between "abolish" and "cancel," there is a world of difference, specifically structural difference. In light of debates—currently raging in the UK due to legislative and regulatory developments affecting higher education—about balancing the competing rights to freedom of speech and freedom from harassment and discrimination, it is imperative to consider what an abolitionist perspective could bring as an alternative or disruption to a liberal human-rights-based framework. Specifically, the notion of "abolition democracy" posed by W. E. B. Du Bois and developed by Angela Davis argues not simply for the destruction of systemic racism but for the (re)construction of new democratic forms and institutions. Only when the structural conditions that marginalize certain voices are overcome will free speech for all be thinkable. This is an axiomatic statement—one that is frequently denounced by the illiberal center and right as dogmatic or at least hyperbolic. The injunction to abolish raises the important question of the limits and necessity of "dogmatism," especially in relation to the critical disposition associated with academic freedom as a category distinct from free speech. There are irresolvable tensions between the institutional-disciplinary legitimacy that underpins professional conceptions of academic freedom, which preaches open-mindedness while determining the bounds of expertise and authorized inquiry, and the urgency of anticolonial modes of critique, which speak in dogmatic, even apocalyptic tones to demand an end to systemic closures. These tensions assume a heightened register when approached through the lens of listening and audibility. This is because aurality is fetishized as bearing an intimate affinity with openness and being-with even as it finds ways to mishear.

No Planetary Future without Re-Attuning Our Ears!
It is not only human rights but humanism tout court from which listening needs to be freed. A logic according to which human rationality is predicated on the distinction between an articulate voice and mere animal noise readily translates into the stratification of human voices, with some dismissed as more *bête* than others. It is not only the voice, though, but a humanist conception of listening that produces inequality, oppression, and the destruction of the planet. The humanism to be abolished is defined not simply by an exceptionalism or anthropocentrism but by a determination of the human as the object of its own teleological production or by some proper essence. Changing migration patterns, warming oceans, and declining biodiversity are, of course, all perceptible to human ears, sometimes with the aid of technological prostheses. Instead of holding on to a distinctly human listening as an (ontologically privileged) exemplar of listening in general, another thought experiment imposes itself: what becomes of listening after human extinction? In the early stages of writing this book, London—like large

parts of Europe—was in the midst of a prolonged and historic drought, and wildfires raged in multiple parts of the Global North, as if nothing else would force us to hear the alarm of planetary catastrophe. If our attunement to the world around us is to bring about meaningful change by giving that world a voice, it is from the standpoint of a listening after extinction, an extinguished human listening, freed from humanism at the same time that it confronts its consequences. It is from this *free listening* that we must take our cue if there is to be any world or any listening left.

Free Listening

1

Silencing Listening

When someone launches a tirade about their being canceled from the front pages of a newspaper or a primetime TV interview, one might smile, bemused, or even scoff, rolling one's eyes. Surely, they can see the irony when they have such a huge platform, one might think. Or one might quote-tweet their performance of outrage with #NoRightToAPlatform, followed by a sad-face emoji. Under most legal regimes, there is no right to be platformed as such. In the UK it would risk infringing on free-speech rights only if the person had been no-platformed in the sense of being either disinvited or blacklisted on the basis of their views, beliefs, or record of lawful expression. This is because, as a key case establishes, platforming extends not only to those who had been invited to speak but also to those whose invitation would be in contemplation.[1] In contemporary parlance, though, use of the term "canceled" is not limited to rescinded invitations, blunt embargoes, or talks that do not go ahead but extends to situations in which desired invitations are not forthcoming or to any form of censure or opprobrium from those deemed to have the authority or power to shape discourse in particular spaces or public debate as a whole, from universities to "the woke mob."

Amid these clamors of "cancel culture" it can become

increasingly difficult to sort through the weeds to identify genuine cases of unwarranted restrictions on freedom of expression
or academic freedom. Knowing where to draw that line between
crying wolf and silencing is part of the problem. At first blush,
it might appear to be a matter of ideology, of political struggle
over the boundaries of acceptable speech, or the effects of new
waves advancing civil liberties and evolving liberation movements. But these political struggles or ideological differences
do not intervene from without on some foundational principle
of free speech. What I hope to show in this book is that those
battlegrounds are symptomatic of the very character of freedom of expression and of liberty more broadly. So long as one
grounds the political subject in freedom-as-liberty, it ineluctably
follows that politics becomes the site of antagonisms over drawing the boundaries of that liberty in a pluralist society. It then
becomes difficult to view debates over freedom of expression as
anything other than periods of historical progress and retrench-
ment, revolution and reaction. The tolerance of the majority,
its limits tested by the clamor of minority voices to be heard,
becomes the barometer of "acceptable" free speech. Looking to
the courts to protect rights that are yet to find favor or begrudg-
ing recognition in majoritarian consensus is likely to result in
disappointment (or fury) insofar as they are institutions that by
design uphold the status quo (or, in some countries, seek to take
us back 150 years). The alternative of a normative, suprahistorical principle of justice—however appealing to some looking
for a less fractious discursive space and ultimately perhaps for
an end to politics dissolved into ethical injunction—comes up
against its own line-drawing dilemmas. Those looking for the
new U.S. university presidents, the new director for freedom of
speech and academic freedom at the Office for the Students in
the UK, or even the case law of the European Court of Human
Rights to give categorical guidance on which words or phrases

are protected speech, in the name of moral certainty, are apprehensive of the potentially infinite responsibility that comes with the task of discerning judgment. Those looking for guidance would seemingly rather settle for entrenched power than take the risks that a more radical pursuit of justice and equality would entail. They want to silence the noise.

Whether more material or metaphysical in their conception, notions of free speech continually contend with a seeming aporia: that its very freedom is premised on binding itself. In this first chapter I'll work through a series of these liberty-curtailing maneuvers to justify my argument for (the necessarily incomplete task of) liberating free speech from liberty and liberalisms of all stripes, and even beyond that from metaphysics and from humanism. Moreover, as I shall set out, this will necessitate liberating free speech *from speech*. That is to say, free speech cannot become free, cannot free itself from its debilitating strictures, unless it substitutes for itself what I am calling *free listening*. This move will also entail liberating listening from its bondage and subordination to speech. None of these liberations, as we shall see, can be a once-and-for-all escape from bondage. Nor is there a predetermined program for liberation. The task of the abolitionist approach I develop by the end is an infinite labor, a renewed commitment, a repeated decision in each instant collectively to destroy the bonds of liberty.

Have I already conceded the battle? Have I too readily ceded the terrain of an essential liberty and critical value to conservatives and reactionaries? No, this book is no white flag of surrender. It's pulling the rug from underneath the feet of those who would exclude, oppress, and dominate in the name of liberty. This book argues conversely that in order to steal a march on their reactionary opponents, those who champion progressive politics should focus instead on the conditions of (im)possibility of free speech and claim the more radical mantle of *free listening*.

This slogan—the book's title—deliberately offers itself to be heard in multiple ways. "Free" can be understood either as an adjective to describe the kind of listening that would be, rather than unfettered or autonomous, *unconditional* in ways this book sets out, while also observing how listening is already in the process of undergoing deconstruction and hence is conditioned and conditional in every moment of freedom. Or "free" may be heard as an imperative—an injunction, a demand, a rallying cry—to create modalities of listening that would genuinely be liberating for all, precisely by liberating practices of listening from not only carceral capitalism but also multiple forms of liberalism and the exclusionary and sometimes racist logics that they abet or continue to encode.

To free listening also means to detach it from—or at least to loosen and renegotiate its relation to—its conceptual determinations, whether that be in the history of political philosophy or in contemporary political rhetoric and practices. It further means to allow it to escape judgment, to relocate it without, and allow it to dislocate any dogmatism or moralism. To approach these liberations, what listening is exactly, and its status as an unequivocal good or panacea for the ills of alienation and polarization, its plethora of contested epistemic or ethical virtues and vices must all be put in question. To this end, it is important to expose how, in a repeated gesture of separating itself from the sphere of aurality, political philosophy reenacts a Platonic moralizing posture. Listening is messy, rowdy, hard to control. It makes those bids to draw clean lines around liberty a complicated business and perhaps ultimately impossible. Free speech in political thought became unfree the moment that it was premised upon the suppression of its aural counterpart— the moment listening was, yes, "canceled."

Cancelations sometimes happen because securing speech is too costly, whether that is because a speaker is likely to attract violent protest or because minority voices incur too great a personal loss in speaking out. Finally, then, to make listening free is to take away its cost, not in the sense of burdening universities and student unions, rather than event organizers, with the bill for hiring private security (as the UK government has legislated) but to liberate it from burden, debt, and guilt, and as such to make it beyond the regime of private property, part of the commons, something that is never my own but comes from the other as apostrophe, as invitation, as warning, as rebuff, as welcome, as rejection—in short a kind of "hostipitality" in Jacques Derrida's neologism in which hospitality is inseparable from the risk of a hostile reception.

The recognition of this risk isn't a carte blanche for racial slurs or deliberate misgendering, for I maintain in this book that it is impossible to free listening without untying that first term—whether as adjective or injunction—from the binds and hostilities of a colonial, patriarchal humanism. Listening, as it is elaborated in this book and developed in some of my earlier work, is, in contrast with the canonical texts of the European political tradition, a decolonial-feminist practice. It is a set of related, though disseminated and potentially contradictory, practices that forge alliances and new ties across struggles and across species without falling back on an ultimately Eurocentric, ostensibly posthuman, postracial universality. The irreducible risk that speech be misheard or go unheard is neither an alibi for unmerited hostility nor an argument for uncritical assent. Rather, it demands that listening be ever vigilant, moment to moment. It demands that each time it must take a position, take a side, make a punctuating response in an act of response-able but incalculable freedom that excepts—or frees—me from myself.

Let us return to our victim of "cancel culture" in *The Telegraph* or on *Fox News*: What exactly have they been denied? What has been "canceled"? If not their expression as such, it is their perceived right to a specific audience that has been stymied or, more generally, even if their ideas are undeniably getting an airing, they lack a *hearing*. Take, for example, an academic who wants to bewail that decolonizing the curriculum is leading to the degradation of academic standards and vents their frustration in the right-wing media. Is that because he has failed to convince colleagues who find his arguments lacking or that they have in effect been foreclosed from discussion in faculty meetings? At what point would we say he has been "heard"? In some sense free speech turns, following J. L. Austin's speech-act theory, on the successful (though maybe not *wholly* successful) performance of an act whose efficacy lies somewhere between mere saying and persuasion but that the author feels has somehow been thwarted in this instance.[2] Much ink has since been spilled on the performative act characterized as "illocutionary," sitting between the locutionary dimension of saying something and the perlocutionary effect produced by saying it. The domain of the perlocutionary is concerned with the consequential yet much less predictable effects on the audience: Will colleagues pay no heed, berate him about his use of racial stereotypes, mollify him by pulling back from some of the more radical proposed changes, engage in fierce debate, or lodge a complaint behind his back? Meanwhile, the scope of the illocutionary—of what one does in saying something—even if it is more constrained in time and variety of effect, is no easier to disentangle from listening. This is because Austin maintains—and this is a point that has provoked much consternation among philosophers— that illocutionary acts require for successful performance "the securing of *uptake*."[3]

How exactly is one to define "uptake" if it is to create a sharp boundary around (successful) illocution and in particular how to distinguish it from perlocution? Austin characterizes uptake as the listener hearing what is said and taking it "in a certain sense." Following Austin in not reducing the "taking as" straightforwardly to "listening," Mary Scudder, in her recent book on listening and deliberative democracy, takes "uptake" to mean hearing plus "fair consideration" (occasionally "due consideration") beyond mere inclusive participation.[4] Although she sometimes describes listening as entailing the performance of a "willingness and desire to take up what others have to say" and "acknowledgement" of their right to have that say, she also stipulates that mere listening, or the auditory act alone, is a necessary but not sufficient condition for the uptake indispensable for democracy. Rather, this requires the successful performance of what she dubs an "ilauditory act" as a complement to Austinian illocution.[5] For Scudder, following Doyle W. Srader's account of performative listening, hearing someone *out* is the sufficient condition for successful performance of an ilauditory act.

There are alternative readings, however, of the uptake requirement in what has become a matter of considerable philosophical debate. As Guy Longworth discusses, at one end of the spectrum, uptake might mean little more than saying something with reasonable communicative intentions, but a stronger version—reflecting the fact that communicative intention, to some extent, entails audience-directed intentions and thus already anticipates listening—would be that one's intentions must be recognized, or slightly weaker, simply recognizable by a (reasonable) listener.[6] This recognition might be of the fact that the speaker is saying something or simply that they are *attempting* to do so, or, with a lesser degree of sensitivity or responsiveness to illocutionary effect, they might simply be taken as or understood as saying something, regardless of any further effects that may have on the listener, who may still choose to forget or reject what is said. It is sometimes argued that these difficulties in delimiting the illocutionary point to the fact that speech acts—and hence freedom of speech—presuppose a horizon of reciprocity. On this reading, "canceling" would consist in depriving a speaker of that minimal listening by which they could reasonably be taken as saying, or attempting to say, something. For example, they might be taken as objecting to decolonizing initiatives.

Note crucially that this analogical logic of taking *as* does not require according respect, giving a *fair* hearing, or any willingness to accept what is said in part or whole. A distinct kind of listening enters the picture once understanding what someone says is no longer a matter of taking it to have been said but of engaging with what is said, of minimally *entertaining* the idea or proposition that saying makes available. This comes closer to the idea of giving expression consideration or a hearing, for example, by weighing the arguments made against decolonizing. It is perhaps only a short step to entertaining an idea and hence to putting the listener in a position of being open to persuasion and, in the absence of contraindications, only a few more steps on the way toward acceptance of what is said: it arguably opens the door for the opponent of decolonizing to win over some of his colleagues. In some cases, it would appear as if the effect of getting the listener to know, realize, heed, or do something is already "built into" the act of saying itself.[7] For example, if an exercise of freedom of expression were to involve urging listeners to do something, or warning or informing them of something, it would appear that that exercise could not be said to be successfully performed without the listener in some way having taken on board or minimally engaged with the content of the urging or warning. Even if they were not to act on it, they would still have been warned, informed, or urged. If our critic of decolonizing were specifically urging colleagues, for example, not to agree to student requests, at what point, beyond the mere auditory act of hearing the words, would they be said to have been urged? It is unclear whether all such cases are properly described as illocutionary. If for uptake it were sufficient to take a speech act as a mere *attempt* to inform—in which case the speaker might not in fact be informed of actual knowledge but could be mistaken or even mendacious—this would be insufficient for the successful imparting of knowledge, as Longworth observes.[8] Listeners cannot be said to have been informed of, for example, data on exam performance that our critic does not know when citing them.

While these may seem to be obscure philosophical debates, they touch on how we might understand complaints of "cancelation" even where a (sizable) platform exists. This idea, like speech-act theory, presupposes that expression has a certain efficacy that in some sense belongs to the speaker. Handing over a degree of responsibility to the listener immediately curbs the autonomy of this capacity. Some types of illocution would appear to depend to a greater extent on the listener's cooperation. Does informing or warning a listener, for example, demand of them more than minimal uptake? Would they, at a minimum, need to have an understanding of what they were being urged to do? And is this a reasonable condition of free speech in a democratic society? Alternatively, is it preferable to consider that this kind of speech requires nothing more of a listener than mere hearing as auditory perception or even that it is reasonable to assume that they can hear in this sense whether they do so or not? *You have been warned, whether you take it in or not!* And yet, for the most part, opponents of "cancel culture," unsatisfied with license to shout into a void (or echo chamber), are more concerned with whether the force of their speech somehow registers with an audience more than minimally, whether it is lent consideration and even credibility—in short, does it get *a* hearing? The suspicion that he has not obtained a hearing among his colleagues is, after all, what motivates our opponent of decolonizing to write in another forum.

To make this hard-to-specify distinction between illocutionary and perlocutionary is already to broach what threatens the very freedom of free speech. In the examples of warning, informing, and so forth whose effect appears to be prescribed in the saying—rather like a promise merely waiting to be fulfilled or broken but whose content isn't otherwise open to renegotiation—there is a determinate or necessary possibility. What distinguishes perlocutionary from illocutionary effects, by contrast, is *another* possibility without which, the opponents of cancel culture appear to suggest, speech isn't sufficiently free: that of the perlocutionary.

There is an inherent tension here. One demands to be at liberty to say whatever one wants, and yet what one can do in speaking depends on listeners to play their part, whether that is simply to hear or to listen, now thinking of the latter as an intensification of sense perception in the direction of attentiveness or receptivity (although there are other ways to configure the logical priority of the two, as we'll address in due course). While some have suggested that the boundary between illocutionary and perlocutionary effects is drawn by the extent of the speaker's responsibility (for the reactions of his colleagues, for example), it would seem both nonsensical and undesirable, from multiple standpoints, to grant free speech immunity for any consequences that exceed determinate possibility (a colleague tears down a statue in response to hearing the criticisms of decolonizing). The law typically draws the line at the reasonably foreseeable. Daniele Lorenzini proposes more radically that a speaker bears a "perlocutionary responsibility" for opening up the more unpredictable, open-ended, conversational, or improvisatory space, by which they might be held morally if not legally accountable for at least some of the indeterminate effects that ensue.[9] From this, Lorenzini persuasively argues that responsibility is itself not a once-and-for-all matter but something open to potentially infinite renegotiation. I would go further: Far from assuming blame for any and every consequence, unconditional responsibility—to use Derrida's term for that ideal in the name of which one exercises only very much conditioned and conditional responsibility—entails that one decide anew each and every time without prescription or calculation in advance. One's responsibility is *not already decided*. To deploy a formula that Derrida often uses to convey his sense of unconditionality, the only responsibility "worthy of the name" is one that, uncertain of its outcomes or rectitude in advance, must take the risk of being a little bit unworthy or irresponsible.

Listening's role in performative efficacy has led to more widespread recognition of, and an expanding body of work on, the notion of "illocutionary silencing," whereby a listener's prejudice or the structural conditions of domination that shape listening practices cause speech acts to misfire for lack of uptake or the credibility (and hence audibility) of the speaker to be undermined among listeners—both of which can further deter them from speaking in the first place for fear of these adverse impacts.[10] These effects quite plausibly have larger ramifications for the entire sphere of free speech and debate insofar as they impair the sharing of a sufficient diversity of knowledge to test and refine ideas. However, the undecidability introduced by listening's co-implication in speech acts makes some nervous about the consequences for free speech. If the efficacy of free speech depends on uptake or some other form of response in one's audience, the fear is that it holds speech hostage to the "perversity" of listening. That a speaker's autonomy in determining their own speech is restricted in this way could have undesirable consequences, the argument goes, such as when a woman's refusal to give consent turns on whether it is recognized or recognizable as such to the speaker, potentially jeopardizing efforts to hold listeners accountable for their culpable failings to listen or understand.[11]

This obtains only if one tethers responsibility to notions of a sovereign subject and of teleology. Indeed, speech act theory and its progressive advances in recent years, even where they give weight to the role of listening as uptake, continue to presuppose an illocutionary act *in potentia*—a capacity or power of performance—logically prior to any response and of which listening amounts to legitimation or fulfilment. Listening can at most cause a performative to "misfire." To this extent, listening remains supplementary and subordinate to speech, rather than its positive condition of possibility. It merely actualizes an existing potentiality. The long European political-philosophical tradition has tended to put aurality in the shadows of voice as its after-echo, often wary of its (politically) destabilizing effects. My contention is thus more provocative than any version of the uptake condition or perlocutionary responsibility. Listening, as what opens up the possibility of free speech, is just as likely to thwart it and be its condition of its *im*possibility. That is because it is the very appeal or call from the other that makes room for speech. This also means that listening's misdirection—the risk of taking what is said as something else, of taking it elsewhere, even of stopping it in its tracks—is not an accident that happens to speech but something that already attends (to) it, makes it what it is, makes it *free* from the very outset, albeit in a sense rather different from performative freedom. To free listening from its reduction to a rubber stamp requires disabusing the notion of free speech of a certain fiction, namely that frank and true speech isn't necessarily susceptible to deceit, error, misdirection (all of which become nigh impossible to regulate once speech is approached from the standpoint of listening). As soon as—better, even before—one has started speaking, listening has already been at work, regardless of whether one addresses an audience or is overheard. It's in the ears of listeners that expression wanders and errs. It's already led my words astray as you readlisten, as Hélène Cixous might say. It's already dissimulating the truth of what I say. But this isn't to lay the blame at listening's door for somehow sullying pure speech; rather insofar as speech is already co-implicated with listening, listening is another name for the waywardness of speech—a waywardness shared by thinkers as unalike as Derrida and Saidiya Hartman.[12]

This experiment in a freedom that one cannot possess, for it comes from the other, moreover entails a response-ability to the other that comes before any culpability or duty. To be free, neither speech nor listening is *owed* to the other as if it were a debt that could be discharged. Listening is a good metaphor for this non-sovereign responsibility in that it suggests an attunement toward the other and toward justice that cannot safely dispense once and for all with errancy but that remains vigilant to what *may* take place. The kind of listening I have in mind and seek to develop in chapter 6 could be said to come "in the wake," as Christina Sharpe puts it, provided this *après-coup* is understood as a *nachträglich* rebounding on any purported origin.[13] Alive to care and repair, attentive to grief, yet as troubling and unsettling to these and other categories as the disturbance of air it follows, it ushers in forms of testimony for which aural vigilance is an enabling condition.

That listening has already rebounded on the sovereignty of free speech, not simply interrupting its performance but ruining it in advance, is evident from the way in which the seemingly self-determining performative presupposes a taking *as*. This *as* means that a speech act *is* only insofar as it is divided and dispersed by the analogical displacement of taking as. Listening has always already dislocated illocution. If a listener understands the speaker *as* saying something other than what they intend to say, they might thereby entertain and even be persuaded by a different proposition. There is no listening or speaking that does not run this risk of wayward mishearing or of being overheard by the wrong person. Speech is only free, only capable of its own power and efficacy, only immune from cancelation to the extent that it is irreducibly delivered over to, suspended over, hanging on the ear of the other. It is not simply that listening adds a prosthesis or series of prostheses onto the end of speech but that this relay is articulated right into the heart of the sovereign performative. Whereas we tend to think of the content of free speech as a proposition that is before a subject that they can seize and put forth, imagining free speech from the standpoint of listening means recognizing that it comes, as David Wills would say, from *behind*, as an off-stage apostrophe that, in pricking up the ear, animates the entire oral-aural circuit of vociferation.[14] If there is any sovereignty worth rebuilding amid the afterlives of slavery or worth defending for Indigenous peoples, it does not fall incident to a subject on the Eurocentric model of self-possession but happens only in and as the wake of a listening that already cuts across and spaces it out.

By calling it an apostrophe I'm already hinting that listening is a *figure* and, therefore, that listening introduces many of the same dilemmas posed by rhetoric for the theory of democracy. Beyond this, listening troubles the entire philosophy of liberty in all its diversity. On the standard account, it is democracy that sets limits on liberty, leading to an interminable calculus of balancing freedoms against one another. My argument, by contrast, is that by virtue of this iterability that aurality installs at the origin, freedom is as much its own condition of impossibility as it is the self-realization of potentiality. That is to say that freedom necessarily constrains, determines, dominates itself (depending on which version of liberty one endorses). Free speech isn't subjected to cancelation. It cancels itself—and it's necessarily possible that it do so.

If cancel culture appears to be symptomatic of certain kinds of (censorious) listening, it is only a short step to saying that the mere fact of listening (of whatever kind)—insofar as it makes the power of speech, to some minimal degree, dependent on the ears of the other, if only for affirmation—has the capacity to cancel speech, to render it unheard or inaudible. But my argument isn't that listening bridles speech but that speech is cancelable to the extent that it is determined as free. Whether freedom is defined as freedom from necessity, from interference, or from domination, it finds its apex as *causa sui* in the modern self-determining subject, absolute in its autonomy, circling back on itself. And yet it is this very absolute that annuls itself, for it must enclose its absoluteness. Consider, for example, as Jean-Luc Nancy suggests, that I can never be absolutely alone, absolutely free, in that I experience myself as alone, as completely free of determination and encumberment, precisely in comparison with those who are not.[15] What would be the experience of solitude if that were all there were? There would accordingly be no experience of freedom without relation to unfreedom. In this sense freedom cancels itself: Too much freedom to the point of being absolute would mean no more freedom, for it would evaporate *as freedom*.

If the history of liberalisms consists in various bids to delimit freedom of expression according to various principles (harm, equality, fairness, truth, and so on), it thus reverberates with this aporetic condition of freedom which, regardless of whether it is figured negatively or positively, individual or republican, repeatedly sutures liberty to listening as a name for its undoing.

Liberalisms have been searching for bulwarks against listening to guarantee that it stays at the margins, which means that they repeatedly find ways to contain liberty within one dark margin or another. As such, the history of liberal thought is one of a series of competing *determinations* of freedom. It pins freedom down, nails it to its mast, stigmatizes it. The hypothesis in this book is that freeing listening is co-extensive with the task of freeing freedom from freedom, that is, from how the history of European thought has *understood* freedom—which might also be to say how it has taken that concept, how it has *heard* it, and thus how a certain kind of listening has already been determining the freedom it would appear belatedly to have infringed. Instead, then, of a cancel culture that curbs or impinges upon sovereign self-determination belatedly from outside, the abolitionism at the culmination of the book's argument in chapter 7—a form of abolition democracy, as W. E. B. Du Bois and Angela Davis set out—would consist in not simply freedom from slavery, oppression, and domination but the destruction *and reconstruction* of the institutions and practices, including liberalism, political thought more broadly, and transcendental philosophy beyond that, whose ideas have determined freedom and, in so doing, have rendered one (person's) freedom subordinate to, at the expense of, in the debt of, weighed in the balance of another('s).[16] Free listening means a new, riskier economy of listening liberated from determination and calculation.

2

Listening at the Margins of the Philosophy of Liberty

Democracy and its freedoms are, at bottom, arguably a problem of counting, of calculating, of distributing, and of having to measure equally what is different. It is in the name of counting equally that democracy appears to curb freedom, as if it were democracy that set limits on liberty. In the classic Millian conception of liberty, it does suffice that it would be for my good, the speaker's, or anyone else's, or that it would prevent immoral conduct; "the only purpose for which power can be rightfully exercised over any member of a civilised community, against his will, is to prevent harm to others."[1] In addition to discarding mere moralism or paternalism, Mill also, therefore, finds it necessary to delimit harm by distinguishing it from mere offense. "If the test be offence to those whose opinion is attacked, I think experience testifies that this offence is given whenever the attack is telling and powerful, and that every opponent who pushes them hard, and whom they find it difficult to answer, appears to them, if they show any strong feeling on the subject, an intemperate opponent."[2]

As jurisprudence on both sides of the Atlantic suggests, drawing these lines—identifying the point at which offense ends and harm begins—is a complex and arduous task and is highly context dependent. In June 2020, for example, a woman was asked by British Transport Police to cover up the t-shirt she was wearing at a Black Lives Matters protest, which bore the slogan "Fuck Boris." Police cited section 5 of the Public Order Act 1986, which prohibits "threatening or abusive" expression within sight or earshot of someone likely to be caused harassment, alarm, or distress. The provision sued to extend to merely "insulting" expression until the government was pressured to drop this descriptor in 2013 after objections on free speech grounds. In this case, perhaps because of the high degree of criticism the European Court of Human Rights expects those in public office to withstand, the police were forced to offer a formal apology, even if in other contexts the same words have been held to be capable of being abusive. Mill would probably think that even in its current form, section 5 risks capturing cases of intemperate offense that fall short of harm.

These moving lines between offense and harm, abuse and insult, threat and political criticism are more than matters for legal adjudication. The law not uncommonly adopts principles sensitive to the vicissitudes of majoritarian opinion on what constitutes harm or abuse, even if, by its nature, it remains less sensitive to ongoing political struggles that show up, as chapter 3 explores, as mere "noise." Mill's insistence on individual autonomy aims to safeguard liberty from the tyranny of a censorious majority. Arguing that protection is needed against "the tyranny of the prevailing opinion and feeling," he observes that "the majority, or those who succeed in making themselves accepted as the majority: the people, consequently, *may* desire to oppress a part of their number; and precautions are as much needed against this, as against any other abuse of power."[3] In adjudicating between unjustified censorship and protection from various harms, the law is, in some sense, playing catch up to sophisticated and evolving debates on the scope and nature of harm in contemporary globally networked societies and, especially within philosophy, on the various epistemic harms that may result from a more or less categorical approach to expressive liberties. As such, the harm principle remains open to often vociferous renegotiation and the border with offense radically unstable. It might seem fairly straightforward to identify incitement to violence, although this has been notoriously contested in "rap on trial" cases, for example, where the conventions of the genre mean that the lyrics cannot be interpreted literally. Determining whether expression amounts to harassment is often far less straightforward. As discussed in chapter 6, research also suggests that harm can be caused by racist or misogynist jokes or slurs, for example— both directly to minorities whose self-image and confidence is adversely affected and indirectly, since demeaning them in the eyes of others fosters discriminatory attitudes.

Moreover, Millian presumptions against the censorship of untrue, immoral, or offensive speech, with the aim of safeguarding the sovereignty of liberty from all but the most minimal interference required, actually rely on arguments about interdependency and as such anticipate the role of listening. Setting aside issues of illocutionary silencing and testimonial justice for one moment, it might appear at first blush that there were good epistemic reasons to set limits on expression that is patently false; witness the fierce debates about dis- and misinformation, at whose doors blame for political polarization and all manner of undesirable electoral outcomes is frequently laid. Such expression, as Quassim Cassam has argued, is all too often mischaracterized as indifferent to the truth or epistemically insouciant when it is, in fact, more accurately recognized as pernicious propaganda that is very much concerned tactically with the truth for its efficacy. There is, notwithstanding this danger, an oft-made argument that it is epistemically preferable for the veracity of ideas to be put to the test of debate.[4]

Some, naively perhaps, put their faith in the "marketplace of ideas" as an enormous sorting hat that would separate true from false, but to the extent that such an economy, like the counting dimension of democracy, is not discriminating as to the quality of idea, this risks simply substituting popularity for criticality. It is on this point that academic freedom of expression distinguishes itself, for example, if only for the reason that it advertises and is presumed to bear an informed authority and imprimatur of legitimacy that warrant greater scrutiny and responsibility. A stronger argument, considered in greater detail in chapter 5, might be made for the academic sphere that, rather than attempting to exclude only what is false, one might more effectively restrict expression of ideas that is not amenable to critique, refinement, correction. It has been suggested that even in the wider public sphere, a presumption against no-platforming ought not hold for speech that seeks only to bedazzle or manipulate, or is otherwise epistemically malevolent.[5] Policing this by drawing lines between, say, intellectual virtuosity and sophistry would be very challenging in practice and at risk of reproducing disciplinary gatekeeping, with dissent or critique mischaracterized as epistemically vicious or otherwise deficient. My larger point, though, is that it is structurally untenable to maintain such distinctions *as a matter of principle* because listening's co-implication renders all expression liable to such perversions. What might be argued instead is that expression that forecloses anything beyond simply affirming its performative force or not (and that thereby cuts out or reduces listening to a rubber stamp) is, in some sense, lacking response-ability. If all I can do is agree or disagree, then the scope of my freedom to respond otherwise or to continue the discussion is restricted in advance. One of the most compelling reasons for allowing the free circulation and deliberation of false ideas is that it is an antidote to dogmatism, insouciance, closed-mindedness, and arrogance, and that it instead contributes to cultivating epistemic virtues of humility, rigor, circumspection, and tolerance of doubt—in short, to the freedom and responsibility that comes from the other and for which listening is one name.

Mill argues that it is important to prevent even true convictions from becoming dogmatic. This is because what matters from an epistemic point of view is not merely whether one has a true belief but whether one has *reasons* for doing so.[6] For Mill that justification depends upon good deliberative capacity, which, in turn, is sharpened through vigorous discussion with diverse interlocutors ("He who knows only his own side of the case, knows little of that").[7] In short, the classic Millian argument against censoring false speech obtains precisely because one of the chief goals and goods of free speech—something like justified conviction—turns on listening having already intervened. Speech is free and not under the weight of dogmatism, moralism, or willful ignorance once it has already passed through a minimum circuit of deliberation. How to define the listening at the heart of this irreducible deliberation? This test of credibility or arguability is evidently something more than mere auditory perception or Austinian uptake and more closely approximates something like entertaining a proposition or even giving it fair consideration. Of course, Mill does not contend that expression must already have passed through the eye of this needle, but one can draw the strong inference that it would need to be *amenable* to such deliberation and justification. Without claiming that viewpoint diversity is in itself epistemically virtuous, some contend that ideas are subjected to more rigorous and effective testing when disagreement is advocated from a position of authentic dissent rather than by a professor playing devil's advocate, who might fail to present the best version of the argument.[8]

At the same time, the idea that democracy requires informed

deliberation tends to expand the breadth of epistemic grounds for restricting the scope of that deliberation to the boundaries of liberal rationality. Much discussion about misinformation and regulation of social media supposes that it is possible to make these distinctions between true and false, epistemic vice and virtue, good and bad faith, and so on, in order to ensure people are exposed if not exclusively then at least to a greater proportion of trustworthy sources of information. It is, of course, very tempting—especially from the cossetted crow's nest of the academy—to want to make the conduct of democracy more orderly in this way. The danger, though, is that regulating expression based on its quality could fall into an undesirable dogmatism of its own, open even to authoritarian exploitation, if its own founding principle of epistemic quality were not subjected to the same degree of critique and humility it esteems. Something like a tyranny of right-thinking people (or philosopher kings) is a peculiar kind of freedom. Moreover, it substitutes a rather Platonic ear whose moralism is distrustful of the colorful and noisy hubbub of democratic debate in action (and probably flinches at the word "fuck") for one that is attuned to and can engage seriously with inequalities of power.

All this should put some pressure on the assumption, prevalent in much modern liberal thought, though also traceable back to ancient Greece, that democracy is straightforwardly a bridle on freedom of expression or at least on the courage to tell the truth or speak truth to power, as the slogan goes (though, of course, free speech has myriad political purposes besides punching up and in our times is more likely to be wielded in the service of *conserving* existing power). Insofar as liberty and autonomy are no less essential to its conception, however, the limits of democracy reveal themselves, on closer inspection, not as secondary constraints introduced belatedly on unbridled freedom but as symptoms of an irreducible tension at the very heart of democracy between two competing imperatives: freedom and equality. In his late lectures on the notion of *parrhēsia*—meaning truth-telling or something like frank, open, fearless, or plain speaking—Michel Foucault struggled precisely with making the kinds of distinctions with which regulators of free speech and especially academic freedom of expression contend: how in the democratic sphere to distinguish between truth-telling and rhetorical manipulation, especially when the latter masquerades as frank talking. "Let me tell you how it is" and "I'm not going to lie to you" are stocks-in-trade of certain strands of populist rhetoric that appeal to skepticism about elite displays of competency and the monopoly on the truth that they purport to have.

For Foucault, it is the pervertibility of *parrhēsia* under the conditions of democracy that will lead to their falling out as the popular ear is inclined to reject whatever reproaches, challenges, or exposes the faults of those listening.[9] To this extent, truth is gradually edged out by popular opinion and any frank dissent against prevailing views by flattery or demagogy. The focus-group approach to party-political signaling and platform building falls into this trap of misconstruing an admirable commitment to listening to citizens as a shortcut to telling them what they want to hear, often at the expense of policymaking that addresses their (material) interests and the social, political, or economic basis for their concerns. In this scenario, rhetoric—and specifically the rhetoric of listening—becomes more than a tool for communicating commitments or even for persuading citizens of hard truths and instead, an end in itself, turns into a performance of reciprocal approbation, a placatory conformism that depletes the courage needed for bold political change in the interests of citizens.

Foucault contends, though, that this threat of "bad *parrhēsia*" is symptomatic of democracy in general, not only the cartel-ization of parties and the ensuing anti-system backlash.[10] According to the principle of *isēgoria*, each Athenian had the equal right to participate in the democratic assembly, both to listen and to speak in an attempt to persuade those listening. Something more, though, is demanded of the *parrhesiast*, whose task it is to speak the truth even—and perhaps especially—when that means nonconformist speech that contradicts the powerful or prevailing orthodoxies. As Foucault observes, "Not everybody can tell the truth because everybody may speak."[11] If *isēgoria* upholds the egalitarian limb of democracy, *parrhēsia* (which Foucault at times associates with its Latin translation as *libertas*) stands for the liberty, license, and free will to say what one wishes and however one wishes, and yet this freedom is predicated on a certain difference or distinction, if not of rational argument or *logos* over *phonē*, as Plato would prefer, then of being discerning as to the truth. One is the freedom for anybody to say anything constrained only by popular reception, the other the freedom to say anything unwelcome on the condition that it is true. In this comparison between *isēgoria* and *parrhēsia*, one starts to see the outlines of a modern-day distinction between freedom of expression and academic freedom, two intersecting categories that pull in different directions, driven, as I argue in chapter 5, by different arts or dispositions of listening.

The European political-philosophical tradition since Plato has tended to marginalize aurality on account of its messiness and propensity for perversion, distortion, and disorder. (Hearing is always at risk of becoming overhearing in the double sense of accidentally eavesdropping and reading too much into what one hears.) Against this backdrop, it is striking that Foucault's account of *parrhēsia* puts listening center stage. Even as the concept takes shape in different contexts, from discipleship to democracy, Foucault is constantly at pains to distinguish the *parrhēsia* proper to the philosopher from its moral adversary, flattery, and its technical counterpart, rhetoric. The difference hinges, as Foucault observes when he first introduces the concept in the lecture course of 1981–82, on the effect produced in listeners. Whereas rhetoric aims to persuade and impress upon the listener, philosophy has as its end fostering the care and government of the self, both of the philosopher and of whoever listens to their counsel.[12] At this point and in the pedagogical setting, Foucault stresses this feature of *parrhēsia* above the frankness and freedom of speech that come to the fore in the democratic context, and yet this transformation in the listener demands a minoritarian or dissenting truth precisely because what is widely accepted would "not change the subject's being at all."[13]

This is not, however, a one-way street. The discussions in this and the following year's lecture course make clear that what is said depends significantly on the art and ethics of listening that can be expected. The disciple must listen attentively, with a committed demeanor and self-reflective silences to digest without rushing to respond or quibble. Further, it is "paraenetic" listening—listening related to moral exhortation—that is taking whatever proposition or assertion is made and turning it into a "precept of action."[14] When it comes to political contexts, listening serves as an especially strong condition of possibility for frank speech because it addresses itself to the political will. Unlike rhetoric, which can seize hold of the listener's will in spite of itself and, to that extent, is potentially coercive, the philosopher's *parrhēsia* is defined by the fact that it must "wait to be listened to" and, indeed, "can only exist by being listened to."[15] Without the promise of a "sympathetic ear" and without listening, it remains empty *logos*. Foucault is quite insistent on listening as a necessary condition for such speech. If it "gets its reality only when it can be listened to" and "cannot be a real discourse, cannot really be a veridiction if it is not addressed to someone who wants to listen," the speaker needs to have reasonable confidence in advance that the audience will listen or needs to put their readiness to listen to frank speech methodically to the test—something that Plato says, with reference to Dionysius, is especially useful when counseling tyrants.[16] The test, then, is whether those listening, be it the public or politicians, have an ear for criticism. While philosophy must be capable of telling the truth of politics without prescribing political action, its discourse cannot be collapsed into political rationality. For Plato, for example, it must be the voice of truth and reason, prepared to say "no" to the powerful passions stirred up and allowed to run riot in the constitutional form of democracy.[17]

This critical or dissenting speech, once again, turns on listening in two respects. In the Platonic account, the threat to reason comes from the melodies, harmonies, and rhythms of music and mimetic poetry, which fret the soul.[18] Furthermore, as Foucault tracks Plato's argument, the philosopher is to be attuned to the distinctive voice or *phonē* of any particular constitution and be able to advise whether the voice expressed in a political decision or course of action is genuinely in tune with it.[19] Democracy, however, is irreparably out of tune. The voice of the masses, which Plato likens to the growl of an animal that needs to be tamed, does not, of course, coincide with that of democracy as a constitutional principle.[20] And yet democracy to Plato's mind is flawed because its love of freedom licenses a multicolored bazaar of constitutions from which the citizen may select as he pleases. Plato cannot counsel the Athenians, who are now so far removed from the truth that they are not prepared to listen to his discourse, and he cannot make the true voice of democracy, if there were such a thing, heard amid the din. Foucault follows Plato in attempting to preserve a certain critical distance or autonomy for *parrhēsia* above the noisy fray of democratic antagonism in which anything goes and yet popularity reigns.

Try as he might, of course, Foucault cannot keep rhetoric and persuasion out of it and must concede that *parrhēsia* is an exercise of power that leaves listeners free to agree or obey, so long as they are persuaded, or to follow other speakers whom they find more persuasive.[21] What matters is that *parrhēsia*, even as it makes tactical use of rhetoric, not be governed by its rules.[22] Rhetoric must be both the opponent and partner of frank speech. *Parrhēsia*'s liminal position at the border between philosophical discourse and political rhetoric is, Geoffrey Bennington suggests, part of its fascination for Foucault.[23] As he walks a delicate tightrope in a bid to forge a caesura between good and bad *parrhēsia*, true and false, good and bad faith, sincerity and its imitation, Foucault repeatedly associates the risk of perversion with the risk that is represented by listening: the risk of failing to persuade, of being misunderstood, of one's intentions going unrecognized, of ridicule, or of an angry backlash. This risk would be that of the tactical use of rhetoric coming untethered from the truth and becoming indiscriminating, which leads Foucault to identify the aporia that, while democracy and *parrhēsia* are mutually necessary conditions for one another, democracy also threatens to unravel truth-telling insofar as it emerges in the joust for ascendency over listeners. As we have seen, however, the risk of listening pertains equally to the situation of philosophical discipleship and not only when the egalitarian imperative of democracy is present.

The analysis that the equality limb of democracy curbs the liberty limb might then be revised. It is not that equality as such contradicts freedom but that they come into conflict with one another when both are determined in a certain way. When equality is defined by number—by votes, by majorities, by mere headcount—it reduces the difference from the other that is a crucial component of the freedom to be oneself, which necessarily includes the freedom of differing from oneself. This economy that counts as the same detracts from the singular *each one* (in their alterity from their other) at the core of democratic freedom. At the same time, a leveling universal that subsumes individuals into a homogenizing totality threatens the *each time* of contingency. And it is this couple—contingency and singularity—insofar as they are incalculable and unknowable in advance, that is encapsulated in the notion of the risk of listening. Even though we use the metaphor of voices heard for voting, the frustrations with electoral politics and representative democracy suggest that truly to listen requires turning an ear each time anew without having presumed what will have been said in advance and without taking it as what one already expects to be said, including that it might surprise the speaker.

Perhaps the objection to democracy is not that its distributive equality allows anyone to joust and argue but that it transfers a greater degree of (epistemic) risk to the side of listening. Without an assurance of truth, there is a significant chance that a listener errs in taking something as something or understanding what the speaker knows. Moreover, the good *parrhesiast*, besides telling the truth, is able to inculcate in the listener the capacity to tell truth from falsity. Far from being too egalitarian, democracy, on the one hand, introduces too much freedom (for anybody to say anything), while, on the other hand, failing to liberate listening from prejudice, stupidity, credulity, and so on. Foucault's concern with listening can go only so far in remediating the comparative neglect of listening in the history of European political philosophy. The stubbornness of speech's priority continues to make audibility a function of political voice and of the subjective sovereignty that underpins it.

Consider Jacques Rancière's suggestion that when striking

workers or other groups protesting unequal or unjust conditions are confronted by a dismissive tone from bosses or government, for example, they are to act *as if* they were equal partners to the conversation, no matter what the other party or the wider public might hold. Even where there is not equal distribution of such a power, they are to make a demonstration of their equality as speaking beings on the basis of a common capacity for speech.[24] In short, it is through the performative power of a fictional "as if" that they can make themselves heard. Rancière is nonetheless attentive to the role of perception. In his analysis, the democratic demand is for a more equal *partage du sensible* (share of what is perceptible)—which means a more equal hearing, a more equal share of audibility. Rancière's argument continues, however, to presuppose a division between articulate, politically audible speech and the mere noisy brouhaha that Plato wanted to expel from the city. On this model all expression, however inaudible at present, has the potential for understanding, uptake, and so on. This ignores the fact that it is the very division into *logos* and *phonē*, into what is and isn't audible, that produces domination. Cleaning up speech by eliminating the noise or turning it into signal, even if that were possible, leaves the structure of domination intact, if not actively reproducing it, by following its purifying zeal.

The issue is less the imposition of an external limit on freedom—equality, justice, fairness, consensus, and so on—than the conception of freedom itself as a power or capacity that one can gather to oneself or possess. So long as freedom is conceived as the property of a subject or a power of effectuation, it will continue to be *determined* by that notion of self-determination, of secularized *causa sui*, and hence unfree. Modern political philosophy has recognized a series of external principles that constrain such subjective freedom, extending from harm (in the classic Millian account) through equality to justice, including

Rawlsian fairness as justice, and even consensus, often as a meta-principle for agreeing the content of other principles. It is conspicuous that, even when the pragmatic nature of such principles is acknowledged, there is an inclination to construe them transhistorically. Liberalisms are far from homogenous, and yet there is almost consistently a search for a principle that would sit above the fray. Take Rawls's famous "veil of ignorance," which subtracts the conditions in which people find themselves in order to arrive at a notion of justice purified of the effects of racial, class, and other social antagonisms. Or consider Miranda Fricker's genealogy, which, in a bid to avoid reducing reason to power and to distinguish silencing or refusing to listen for good reason rather than out of prejudice, appeals to a suprahistorical substratum of rationality that persists through modulations of power and thereby functions as normative ground for judgments of epistemic justice and injustice. By contrast, as Lorenzini argues, Foucault's genealogy allows for the cultivation of epistemic virtues such as humility and critical reflexivity even in relation to the foundational norms of rationality.[25]

Grounding the limits of freedom in transcendental conditions thereby embraces the enclosure of freedom within a metaphysical horizon. For a Derridean like Bennington, not even Foucault is immune, seduced as he is by a quasi-Platonic moralizing distrust of rhetoric and hence the fiction of purity: that it would be possible to have frank speech entirely free of rhetoric, manipulation, distortion, and so on (except that the demos wouldn't be prepared to listen). It is this determination or enclosure of freedom that renders it unfree and that is unsettled by refocusing on the differential, dispersive, and unpredictable terrain of listening, for listening is what exposes those grounds not only to criticality but, moreover, to the surprise of contingency. This is neither anarchy nor abdication of responsibility.

What it demands is that a decision on justice be taken *each time*. This means listening in the fuller sense: beyond uptake or understanding something as something, of being open to being unsettled by what the other says. Notwithstanding some of the ongoing debates within Derrida studies on this question, it is not consistent with the deconstruction of the Kantian Idea, which ruins all teleology in advance, with Derrida's doubts about Nancy's appeals to foundational principles like fraternity, or with everything he has to say about the event to suggest that this openness to the other has quasi-normative force or is a quasi-normative imperative.[26] Listening doesn't institute a norm of responsibility (that would compel it to listen in a particular way). If it is to be free, this responsibility cannot be determined in advance by any ethics, by any metaphysics, or even by any humanism, as will be discussed in chapter 7, without such categories trembling. Rather, it is necessarily differantial, caught in antagonism without being dialectically resolvable—in short, the noise and clamor of democracy.

Finally, then, on a further analysis, freedom is not up against an external limit nor is it aporetic for having been composed of two irreconcilable notions pulling in different directions, alternately loosening until it almost unravels and tightening up to the point of suffocation. Rather, democracy is precarious because freedom limits *itself*. Far from coming up against a competing concept of equality, freedom must measure itself and come up short. That is to say, it must apportion, distribute, share itself lest it give too much self-determining force to what it is not and to what would destroy democracy. It must bind itself a little lest it unleash the power of unfreedom. This is why we come up against the perverse consequence that democracy tolerates and grants so much license that it would even tolerate the exercise of freedoms aimed at the very destruction of democracy. It is for this reason that we see self-preserving restrictions in democratic regimes, including legislative provisions such as Article 17 of the European Convention on Human Rights, which precludes anyone relying on Convention rights and freedoms to destroy those rights and freedoms. Modern rights-based democracy thus touches its own limit, granting freedom, but only to the point where it would not be free to destroy itself. Beyond this, the Convention and its jurisprudence, of course, allow freedoms to be further curtailed when carefully balanced against the protection of others' freedoms.

This calculus of freedom is already to determine it. The notion of balancing freedom with other rights or freedoms—of drawing a line where freedom meets constraint, of apportioning freedom and what is other than itself—splits off the opposite of freedom, in all its differential and dispersive nature, into an unfreedom that comes from without (harm, equality, fairness, human rationality, etc.) and thereby enables a fiction—and performative "as if"—about freedom's unity and sovereignty. This fable of freedom distracts from its self-differentiation, from the fact that it tends to divide and differ from itself. The division into an opposition or dialectic stabilizes so as to master that dispersive force. Analyzing the willful subject, Sara Ahmed, for example, describes the way in which the will, which is not only synonymous with freedom but also "invested with the power of checking that freedom" and hence points to a subject at variance or out of joint with itself, is externalized "to preserve a fantasy of interiority."[27] Noticeably this projection takes an aural form, heard as the voice of another who commands. Insofar as listening is one name for the contingency and singularity that infect freedom from the outset and make it shatter in our grasp, European political philosophy has tended to silence it, casting it out to the peripheries of irrationality. To free listening means to liberate it from any determinations that could enclose its chancy, risky, each-time openness: from transhistorical ethical injunctions, from metaphysical foundations that bind the human to a proper essence, from an anthropocentrism that makes of freedom an exclusively human capacity, from a Eurocentrism that consigns alleged madness to the colonized peripheries—all tasks that cannot be accomplished once and for all. Listening is not and cannot be mine. Its scarcely audible tale is one that this book attempts to sound.

3

Captive Playlistening

Cued Up Subjects

After two waves of transformation, musical listening is free. Or at least it is possible to listen to music via online streaming services without handing over cash. Each wave of the revolution in the consumption of recorded music around the turn of the twenty-first century cumulatively rewrote its political economy as it shifted from an ownership to a rental model. As Martin Scherzinger narrates, the nineties and noughties saw a radical decoupling from the commodity form as musical tracks were distributed via informal downloading and file-sharing over peer-to-peer networks.[1] The very mechanisms of this democratization and liberalization of a techno-utopian era, however, were soon co-opted as the basis for a remonetization and recapture of musical labor via the functionality of streaming over high-speed connections. By the 2010s there was a return to the regimes of copyright and licensing, while, at the same time, platforms were reeling in the labor of listening. While many of the main music-streaming platforms, including Spotify and YouTube, operate on a freemium model, musical listening online is not free. It comes, rather, at the cost of surrendering, first, one's aural attention to the interruption and distraction of in-stream advertising and, second, one's privacy to dataveillance of the minutiae of one's listening activities.

Eric Drott argues, in a touchstone article on streaming as a technology of surveillance, that listening data is especially powerful because it offers a window into the user's innermost psyche, capitalizing on music's distinctive capacity as an especially powerful technology of the self.[2] Platformized listening, therefore, intersects in a second way with the adjective "free," directly engaging and recomposing the free subject of modern liberalisms. Much of the popular and sociological critical discussion about music streaming has focused on the impacts on artists and their revenues, but scholars in music studies, from ethnomusicology to music theory, have begun to contend with the ways in which listening to algorithmically curated playlists, in contrast with the DIY or maker cultures of the P2P high-water mark, is radically transforming listening subjects. Some will no doubt object that listening to music is a very different act from listening to others in a democratic-discursive context, and no doubt they should not be carelessly elided. And yet the forms assumed by musical listening today have a significant impact on the modalities of listening available to us as democratic subjects. Any kind of listening, no matter what the object, may form habits, but, more specifically, musical listening recruits and produces political subjects, individual and collective, and, for this reason, provides a crucial backdrop for thinking about the liberation of political listening in the twenty-first century. This is an argument that can persuasively be made from both an anthropological and a music-analytical perspective, although it ought also to be subject to close critical scrutiny since it is inseparable from an aesthetic ideology that sought to locate human freedom in the artwork exalted on high.

Theodor W. Adorno is famous for having clung to such a Romantic view, making the contentious distinction between the kinds of listening elicited by different genres of music. If the music of Beethoven, say, or Mahler is capable of soliciting a structural listening attentive to the unfolding of musical form, he notoriously dismissed jazz and popular music for encouraging listeners to attend, in a distracted fashion, only to the delectations of attractive, decontextualized morsels. Adorno's preference for a listening that could track the making of totality through dialectical synthesis was closely related to his analysis of a certain heroic subjectivity in middle-period Beethoven, especially sonata-form movements, where the musical subject— and, by extension, the listening one—would reach self-identity having faced, overcome, and integrated the adversity of the other. In short, structural listening by which a representation of the totality might be formed was the paradigm of sovereign mastery, self-possession, and auto-affection. This was precisely why it embodied the spirit of both Enlightenment and Revolutionary freedoms. Such listening was, therefore, the ideal vehicle for the production of the modern liberal subject. The reversal of freedom into tyranny, terror, and later technological domination, however, would leave Adorno's late Beethoven able only to register the retreat of subjectivity. The social totality mirrored in heroic listening had been exposed as a lie, and from the rubble all that remains are the embers of a broken subjectivity that could only express something like the Kantian Idea or the Hegelian synthesis in the moment of its fall, like a shooting star. I reprise this well-worn analysis (no doubt too familiar to readers in music studies) to highlight that Adorno is not a hypocrite, as is sometimes assumed, when he reveals a soft spot for *schöne Stellen* or beautiful passages, for these singular, fragile moments in Beethoven and Schubert, for example, attest for him to the impossibility of totality, self-identity, and sovereignty and not to the recommodification of the fragment in a new digital capitalist totality. In short, far from assuring the self-presence of the liberal in possession of its freedom, they are testament to a subject that exists only insofar as it risks itself in the ears of the other who alone can recognize it in the final glow of its embers.

This has not stopped music scholars from adopting the Adornian heroic mode of self-determination as a model for musical listening on personal, portable devices: before cloud-based streaming to our phones and tablets, the iPod and, before that, the Walkman.[3] The link between curated musical listening and selfhood was notably substantiated by Tia DeNora, who, calling music "the commonsense medium *par excellence* of feeling and all things 'personal,'" analyzed its role in the reflexive project of constituting the self, studying ethnographically the various kinds of emotional, memory, and biographical labor that personalized listening puts in motion and how it is mobilized in everyday life to regulate cognitive and affective states and to modulate mood and energy level.[4] Musical listening can be deployed, she found, to sculpt desire, concentration, or motivation, to soothe anxiety, or to channel anger. Musical listening, so her influential argument goes, is a device or resource to forge agency, a vehicle for self-presentation, and a means to construct and repair self-identity. In particular, DeNora's research highlights how listening sutures the "choreography of feeling" with the performance of self. (It perhaps comes as no surprise that her first book was on Beethoven and the social construction of genius and autonomy, nor that her third, after *Music in Everyday Life*, would be devoted to Adorno, including his part in the reception of heroic Beethoven.)

Ethnographic work by Michael Bull on personal devices has observed how users deploy playlists to overlay the spaces around them with their own soundtrack and thereby to rescript their journeys and trajectories in urban space according to their own narrative and affective state. Unlike blasting music from a car so to as make one's own musical tastes a public affair, the mobile listener with earbuds or headphones constructs a private world within public space, often with a protective or empowering function. Above all, these listening practices bestow a sense of subjective efficacy, grounded in the curated playlist, and in this way amount to an exercise of liberal freedom. They free the listeners from the sonic determinations of their environment: the Muzak playing in the shop, the relentless sound of traffic while walking along the road, the noisy conversation on the bus. By producing a mobile personal bubble, they also tend to shield one from interpersonal interactions—in short, from having to listen to the other.

In this regard, mobile listening is a rather different affair from concert listening to canonical works of the Classical style. Even listened to in the privacy of one's home on (audiophile-quality) hi-fi equipment, art music of the late eighteenth century produces an experience of collectivity in a way that the personal sonic overlay of public space does not. This is because, as I have argued in earlier work, the construction of a representation of the musical totality during the course of listening to its unfolding does not simply mirror the production of self-identity but crucially depends upon knowledge of a shared reservoir of conventions—tonal, syntactic, and stylistic—that enable one to anticipate and aid retention.[5] If one recognizes the cadential convention that Haydn misuses to witty ends, for instance, it is on account of a common epistemic world that one can hear internally how the music should or could have gone. If one recognizes the typical tonal maneuvers of a retransition, for example, then one will know to expect the imminent onset of the recapitulation. If a listener can be toyed with knowingly in a coda, it is precisely because they instantly recognize its closing function and are also familiar with the set of strategies that can be deployed to defer it.

This is all to say that certain formal properties of Austro-Germanic music of this period are predominant factors in molding the particular power of attention a listener brings. In what follows, I am interested less in revisiting Adorno's argument that popular music fosters distracted listening or entrenches low-brow appetites than in considering how the affordances of digital streaming platforms themselves elicit modalities of attention and taste, and not only the content they disseminate (although the interactions and potential for boundary-blurring between the two also interest me). But I also want to underscore the ways in which each kind of listening departs from constructing the sovereign individual subject of listening, even as it appears to do just this. A listener to a Mozart string quartet is not only in that particular moment but also going back and forth between earlier and later moments, in order that they might listen to the quartet *as* something, that they might recognize or understand some detail in it *as* something. Something like musical uptake draws upon a whole host of other listenings beyond this shuttling back of remembered and anticipatory hearings. My listenings, on prior occasions, to this and other works related to different degrees to one another but also the listenings of others, which have formed the sedimented layers of commonly understood convention and recognizable deviation. The subject of listening here, if there is such a thing, has already been multiplied, divided, and dispersed in advance. The playlistening subject, too, has none of the illusory unity and self-sufficiency typically accorded to the modern liberal subject of free speech. In this way digital listening practices expose the fundamental condition of listening as something that can never be mine, never in my grasp, and can never leave me identical to myself, but has already apostrophized me and prostheticized me from behind.

Compared with personally curated playlists, whether on a mobile device, on a home stereo, or at a concert one has chosen to attend, the situation is, on the face of it, quite different when the playlist is instead created by a recommendation algorithm, albeit one partly or substantially based on the listener's own habits and online behaviors. That listening, even when solitary, is irreducibly collective is perhaps most palpable in the case of collaborative filtering. The most common recommender technique, dating back to the 1990s, is where an algorithm constructs the list of recommended tracks to be cued up based on patterns of correlations between a list of users and a set of tracks, sometimes in two-dimensional space, often with one axis tracking a demographic attribute. These relations are then mediated by their rankings, usually deduced implicitly from listening and skipping history. In short, the algorithm, even with no particular knowledge about any given listener or about the track, can pick out what listeners "like you" listen to, equating being like with liking the same music. In this way, collaborative recommendation automates the construction of correspondences between individual and aggregate. This is no individual subject of listening. As Nick Seaver argues, "collaborative filtering was not about privileging individuals over broader demographic categories, but about reinstalling isolated individuals into an algorithmically tuned collective."[6] Far from buttressing individuating liberty, such algorithmic recommendation relies upon a quasi-biopolitical probabilistic determination of its listening subjects, always at risk of reproducing the crudest negative stereotyping of minorities. Free listening this ain't.

Content-based recommender systems, such as Pandora's "Music Genome Project," which underpinned its personalized radio stations, sought to address the limitations of collaborative filtering by giving weight to the sonic content itself. This, though, requires sufficiently discerning ears to identify relevant qualities of the music, such as genre, tempo, instrumentation, or formal, rhythmic, melodic, or harmonic features—the equivalent to its DNA in Pandora's metaphor. Pandora's approach of relying on trained human "musicologists," though arguably a selling point for its curatorial prowess, has been seen as too resource intensive, limiting the size of the platform's catalog to the labor time of its listeners.[7] Machine listening trained by human listeners, such as The Echo Nest's system designed in MIT's Media Lab and acquired by Spotify, offers a more cost-effective alternative to expert tagging track-by-track. These techniques of listening mediated through human-machine interactions are unlikely to assuage Adorno's fears, though. Even if there appears to be an element of harmonic analysis and attention to hierarchical structures in The Echo Nest's listening, all the indications are that algorithmic listening is departing rapidly from traditional norms of music-theoretical listening to privilege affective markers in sound, coupled with automated affective content analysis of song lyrics. This accords with the rise of context-based recommendation, which finds correlations between tracks and listening time, location, and probable occasion or activity. The digital listening subject, if there is such a thing, is a far cry from the self-identical modern liberal subject, instead decomposed into data fragments of habit and affect—whence the number of apps that create a custom musical track based upon a facial analysis.[8]

Algorithmic listening recommendation is not far removed from the addictive casino listening that I have analyzed elsewhere, whereby an intermittent reinforcement schedule of winning jingles and clattering coins (even for losses disguised as wins, where players win less or no more money than they bet) plays a key role in keeping the gambler hooked on the promise of a (bigger) win around the corner.[9] Both elicit forms of listening as self-entrapment. The tendencies or compulsions of listeners are enlisted to make them more susceptible to persuasion. The freedom experienced in the will to play again or keep playing is a thinly veiled coercion. This one-more-spin listening, which relies upon the veneer of a voluntary, individual will, entraps insofar as it recruits listeners to play a pre-scripted role seemingly of their own volition or even initiative. Playbor is perhaps always a kind of role- or cosplay. One way to conceive of the subject of digital labor is that they are not human at all but rather a placeholder created as a result of distributed computational process to be occupied by a category of user. It is thus not only tracks but listening subjects that platform playlists have cued up.

When Stéphane-Eloïse Gras argues that music information retrieval algorithms like The Echo Nest have turned into tastemaker machines, not simply descriptive but normative, this not only unsettles the prevailing humanism of the philosophy of aesthetic judgment.[10] Moreover, it suggests that these listening machines are in the business of constructing listening subjects that do not as yet exist. Whereas in the kinds of technologically mediated musical listening discussed by Bull and DeNora the player is a tool or machine at the disposal of a human listener (and, as such, an instrument before them and to hand, ready to grasp), the notion of a machine listening that comes before any human listener challenges us to consider how listening is always already technologized and to put pressure on the categorial opposition of human and technological.

The question is: Who or what exactly are these digital subjects produced by ensemble techniques of machine listening? In various ways, depending on the exact conception, digital subjectivity at first blush appears to offer a challenge to the self-contained and representational subject of metaphysics and liberalism, but whether it offers a politically attractive alternative or a retrograde step is another question. The assumption, followed, for example, by Drott in his dataveillance-centered critique, is that digital subjects are "data doubles" or fragmented Deleuzian dividuals, abstract representations of an individual composed of the aggregated trails of personal data. The focus then becomes the deviation in the flesh-and-blood individual misrepresented (or misheard) and the sociopolitical dangers and potential injustice of associating this partial or fragmented representation with a specific real-world counterpart.[11] Even when it entails multiplication through aggregation, the reduction of the singular life, compounded by dataveillance's intrusion into the privacy of the classical liberal subject, makes for an unpalatable politics for proponents of civil liberties.

More supple conceptualizations of digital subjectivity and subjectivation that break with the metaphysics of presence inherent in representational regimes allow one to analyze how algorithmic listening—whether MIR systems, listening on streaming platforms, affective listening in automated telephone answering systems, or what is known as social listening—exposes the deconstruction of the selfsame subject of liberalism. These more-or-less-than-human (posthuman?) forms of singularity and multiplicity, individualized and personalized yet aggregated and probabilistic, swerve away from the classical modern subject with bodily, phenomenological, and psychological continuity. Luciana Parisi argues that computational sovereignty debunks the subject of transcendental reason as the self-determination of reason disintegrates into the determination of probabilistic algorithms. Whereas industrial capital fragmented the subject by the assembly line and the clock, the platform user is broken down into statistical likelihood expressed in bits. Parisi's analysis looks to the incomputable and indeterminable beyond the programmable, hence suggesting how machine thinking might pose a challenge to the self-positing subject.[12] Specifically addressing sound, Sumanth Gopinath and Jason Stanyek contrast the selfhood at stake in millennial mobile personal listening, with sonic practices in the era of ubiquitous streaming, with what they dub "selfiehood."[13] More palpably recursive and depending on feedback loops, over multiple timescales, that blur the boundary between human and technological as users engage in practices of self-quantification and tracking, selfiehood is nonetheless an extension of the neoliberal project, making participation and creativity available to capital to metabolize.

The nature of the neoliberal subject in general means that its anxious precarity resulting from reconfigured labor markets is transformed into flexibility and adaptability by which the self becomes a personal project of entrepreneurship and betterment—hence the need to capture creativity and sociality—and the risks of capitalism are outsourced to the individual worker.[14] Neoliberalism does not so much break with modern liberalism as it intensifies the *performative* character of the subjectivity it produces. If capitalism is a source of both domination (by the impersonal force of markets and by the subordination of wage labor) and disenchantment (because of alienation under wage labor and what Lauren Berlant calls the "cruel optimism" of its promises of a good life for all), its new neoliberal spirit mobilizes the desire for autonomy and the capacity for initiative, with the result that, via more stringent performance management, the subject's freedom becomes a Weberian iron cage of their own making.[15] The digital extrapolation of neoliberal subjectivation takes this "as if" to a new level, laying it bare. The labor that services the digital economy, which extends the autonomists' notion of social factory in further recognizing the labor of social reproduction beyond the wage, is free in the sense that it is unpaid. It erodes the boundary between production and consumption, while at the time it appears to give the user the benefit of a service at no cost.

Rather, though, than bemoan the gap between fictional performance and the real thing, some media theorists stress the "distance" between the two as constitutive of digital subjects. For Olga Goriunova, for example, this is a Leibnizian distance (or at least Leibniz as read by Deleuze read by media theory), "thick" and "luminous," capable of expansion, contraction, twisting, or other distortion.[16] In fact, the digital subject is formed precisely in the necessary metamorphosis that takes place. Nonetheless, this distance as Goriunova describes it still has an analogical quality: it takes something *as* something insofar as "her" digital subject is still, in some way, recognizable as "her," even if the distance is the terrain of political struggle. The virtue of her analysis is that it makes a site of political antagonism out of the moment of recognition in listening—how something is "heard" *as* something computationally in the sense that algorithms conduct what is known as social listening. The significant drawback to the analysis, however, is that it fails to realize that distance is not "between" real-world and digital but has always already gone all the way into a technologized human subject as a relay of articulations.[17] Unlike a distance that starts at the moment it produces the digital subject, this technological prostheticity has already disrupted and ruined the possibility of the metaphysical self-identical subject in advance.

The digital subject is not straightforwardly other than the living human subject but exposes how life just is technological. In one crucial respect, however, the digital subject has already grasped and determined this prosthetic inanimation by making it a matter of probability, of calculable likelihood. Digital subjects aren't aftereffects or echoes but likely or future candidates for the user. Goriunova claims that users are only interpellated by algorithms insofar as they have been conditioned to hear and answer to this call to the metaphysical subject. She further argues that digital subjects, to the extent that they do not coincide with their data sources or actions, throw a spanner in the works because they challenge existing notions of authenticity and reality. And yet, in much the same way that the notion of the posthuman necessarily presupposes and leaves intact the Enlightenment humanism it purports to transcend, as a specter that haunts from the grave of its alleged historical rupture, the "posthumanites" approach endorsed by Goriunova and other media theorists is too hasty in imagining that it can so readily purify itself of metaphysics.

The reduction to predictability, moreover, threatens to turn the user into the mere rubber stamp of the digital subject's performative potentiality, just as we saw that uptake could be interpreted as the mere actualization of the speech act's predetermined possibility. Mindful of this problem, Scott Wark responds to Goriunova's proposals by arguing that digital subjects, constituted in and as circulating data, are the occasion for their own individuation and that of human users it predicates.[18] The grammars of action on the basis of which digital subjects individuate are shaped less by the sovereign will than by the circulation of aggregated data on human user actions. This circulation is therefore not unlike the system of language or, indeed, of listening that technologizes the human body and mind alike when speech or sound arrives before or even without them, that is to say, from the other—except that Wark is determined to give this technologization a consistency that would earn it the name of "subject." His technical entities (modeled after Gilbert Simondon via Yuk Hui) are subjects insofar as they possess their own (self-)sufficiency, regulating their relationships to other digital objects, the wider digital milieu, and also to themselves. Even if this theory of individuation accounts for mediation and privileges ontogenetic becoming over ontological substantiation, it fails to make any dent on the sovereign subject of metaphysics, because that becoming turns on self-regulation.

To unsettle the fetishization of the subject, one might want to look elsewhere, away from the scenes of recognition and misrecognition and to the production of affect. Drott argues that data from music streaming services are especially valuable because of music's capacity to serve as a technology of the self and the distinctive affective investment users make in music, deploying it to modulate mood and emotion across many different times and places. My interest, however, lies in the capacity of playlistening to provoke feeling without clear teleology or intentionality, or even after the death of the subject, as the title of Rei Terada's book has it.[19] Without subscribing to the traditional affect/emotion distinction, which demands deconstruction, the kind of feeling I have in mind is not the possession of a single phenomenological subject but is irreducibly social, material, even structural in the sense that Raymond Williams famously gave it, though without any periodizing connotations. Like Sianne Ngai's "ugly feelings," the affective states generated by listening on music streaming platforms or being overheard by affective machine listening are uncomfortable and ambiguous, often at least partly unwanted and ill-suited to cathexis or channeling into political projects or action.[20] Ngai contrasts such ignoble feelings with those grand passions that channel affect toward emotion and agency. Irritation is the ambiguous, harder-to-pin-down cousin of goal- and object-oriented anger, envy the petty sibling of jealousy that undermines the objectivity of its object, and hence its own intentionality, by making its distaste of class inequality shameful, and stuplimity the often comically over-excited fatigue that pales in comparison with the awe, terror, and transcendence of the sublime. Ngai, for her part, is interested in aesthetic emotion and develops the notion of literary tone to describe the global affect or general disposition of a text that is reducible to neither the represented feelings of the characters nor the emotional reaction of the reader, whether via empathetic identification or otherwise. To appreciate the discrepancy in the context of musical listening, consider, for example, the sweet sadness cultivated by listening to sad songs from which a listener derives a measure of comfort, even pleasure. But Ngai is thinking of a more significant instability whereby a listener might be uncertain or confused as to whether a feeling is theirs or "in the music."

My suggestion is that playlistening tends to induce precisely this kind of ambivalence and uncertainty. Whereas for Ngai, however, the relation of subjective and objective is dialectical, my contention is that this kind of listening exposes a more fundamental undecidability about the propriety of feeling. Algorithmically designed playlists are tailored to digital subjects, constructed as circulations of aggregated data. As such, the intimate listenings they promise are already social, even spaces of public intimacy. Affect wasn't stolen from the phenomenological subject by post-structuralism. It was never hers. Following the argument I made about listening, the listening subject interpellated by the playlist is constructed before, or perhaps behind, any individual listener in particular, who is technologized in advance, not simply by affect as a prosthetic relay that has always already come from the other. Tone, in the sense that I adapt from Ngai, is the tone of an apostrophizing voice, but not the voice as the possession of a subject, human or otherwise. Tone has some affinity with the notion of vibes (or vibez) elaborated by Robin James in that it breaks with the model of sympathetic resonance that has predominated in discourse about sound and vibration.[21] Rather, in setting a tone, playlistening provides an orientation or horizon of action, cultivating certain sanctioned capacities while excluding or threatening to punish others. For James, vibes are a form of governmentality that relies less on normative imperative than on the speculative calculus that exceeds probabilistic calculation and admits of uncertainty when asking what a Spotify user wants to listen to next.

Feeling after—or indeed without—the subject is not a contradiction, for emotion has long rattled the paradigm of the classical philosophical subject, the same subject of the *logos* jeopardized by the noisy stirrings of democracy. Developing Terada's point, I suggest that passion at once unravels and exposes the secrecy of subjectivity. It undoes intentionality even as it has the structure of all subjection, as (self-)constraint on volition.[22] It's freedom binding itself. Ironically perhaps, it is precisely when algorithmically curated listening purports to be most personalized, to most closely approximate a care of the self, that it unleashes the circulation of a subjective feeling as the driving force of what appears to come from—and to express—the subject. To speak of a dialectic of subjective and objective is already to divide so as to stabilize the proliferating and differential effects of feeling that comes from the other before or in the back of the self. Emotion is the disorienting turn I make in response to the call of that tone.

And yet playlistening wants to appropriate this difference to an illusory phenomenological self, even as it relies upon the fragility of that project to keep listeners on the hook and data for sale. As the wheel keeps spinning, as we skip with increasing frequency, and our mood spirals in a drawn-out, iterable agglutination, it tips over from an affirmative "that feels right" or enchanted surprise into boredom, even mild irritation. One is not just being played music (chosen for one's ear, one's taste), one is *being played* (one's ear, taste, and very self in the making). One might even experience other minor negative affects as a result of the ambivalence felt as the mismatch between listener and digital subject—indeed between the subject and itself— becomes more inescapable and the ongoing search for a source of self-soothing or satisfaction is exposed as plain distraction and procrastination. Even when it does feel just right, the seemingly perfect feedback loop can provoke a navel-gazing boredom due to the lack of surprise, sociality, and difference. Playlists get burned out, and listeners burned out rather than liberated.

It is sometimes suggested that the sheer complexity of big data and black-boxed code induces an algorithmic sublime, but this misses the crucial, all-too-often overlooked second moment of the Kantian sublime, in which human reason enjoys its transcendence and superiority over what, in nature, had initially astonished and overwhelmed the human imagination. Awe gives way to a soaring autonomy of rationality, securing the subject of the Enlightenment and its freedom of self-determination. Like rage, which will be discussed in the next chapter, the sublime is a dramatic, directive, and sharpening feeling, more easily recuperable to a subject, and, as such, it gives rise to a certain serenity of affect. By contrast, in the atonal, noisy tone of ignoble effects studied by Ngai and that I discern in musical playlistening, the lack of willfulness or purpose that all too often sets in is experienced as tedious and, hence, as disempowering. Ngai says "stultifying"; in Kant's vocabulary, they're "languid" rather than "strenuous."[23] The encounter with tone as objective feeling "out there" exposes mood's dependencies, rather than the power of reason. In the end what is sold are not deep affective investments but atonalities about which listeners might well struggle to care, and yet the fact that they don't care is somewhat irksome—a feeling that can only be assuaged again in the hope that the next track will elicit something more like willpower or agency. In a sense, machine listening—both the kind that underpins recommendation systems and also that used to monitor affect in the voice in digital personal assistants, for example—is a means of re- or misdirecting affect to disperse or block the modern liberal subject in ways that might be associated with the political dynamics of both obstructionism and contagion. Insofar as habits of musical listening shape aural possibilities in the democratic sphere, where this leaves passionate utterances—arguably the last resort of the powerless in an increasingly illiberal world—is an urgent question.

4

Listening

It's All the Rage

At the time of first drafting this chapter, the British tabloid press has turned its fire on two Black female professors in the United States, both of whose families were affected by British colonialism, for tweeting intemperate comments at the time of the British monarch's death. Once billionaire Jeff Bezos weighed in, the university at which the first professor worked—and to which Amazon has donated $2 million—issued a statement distancing the institution from the "offensive and objectionable messages" while defending the professor's right to extramural freedom of expression. As the second professor entered the fray to defend her and add her own strongly worded expression of anticolonialist sentiment, the ensuing media storm and attacks on social media, many of them plainly racist and misogynist, were far more immoderate in tone than either of the offending posts.

My point in highlighting this incident is not to adjudicate as such on the line at which the manner of dissenting speech becomes too intemperate or too outrageous (even if I have my own personal view on the matter). As I will argue in the pages that follow, this move itself is deeply problematic for what it says about the rage of the oppressed and its capacity to be heard. While the outrage sparked by Black female dissent was markedly at a higher pitch, white antimonarchists, who were variously critical of the institution's involvement in colonialism or of the antidemocratic nature of hereditary monarchy—especially of the new king's rushed accession, seemingly designed to forestall debate—found themselves intimidated, moved on, arrested, and even charged by police in England and Scotland for moderate expression of criticism, for silently holding placards with republican or abolitionist messages such as #NotMyKing, or even for a blank sign held up by a barrister in deliberate reference to the Hong Kong protests against the national security law. These incidents have sparked outcry about undemocratic crackdowns on protest, especially since republican dissent has been something of a tradition in the UK. The Conservative government, notwithstanding its heated rhetoric about free speech, was quick to introduce legislation that criminalizes noisy or disruptive protest. These incidents have, at the same time, prompted fury from monarchists who have argued that it shows a lack of "respect" or that it is "neither the time nor the place," suggesting a desire to limit freedom of expression by reference to propriety.

This argument over expression's proper affect or figurative "noisiness" ought not be surprising if one considers that the modern liberal conception of free speech has been intimately bound up with the ideology of possessive individualism and with the bourgeois property rights that go hand in hand (and glove!) with class-, caste-, and race-based notions of decorum and fitting behavior. If the goal has always been to dismiss expression dissenting from the norms of the establishment or the otherwise powerful as beyond the pale, what better tactic than to point to a speaker whose animatedness somehow forfeits their right to be part of a certain public space because it offends against sanctioned sensibilities? My interest, though, is less in how dissent from the status quo is framed as inherently uncivil, regardless of whether it's an unspoken f-word on a banner or a supremely articulate white male professional, than in how the policing of tone, manner, and affect is managed via a specifically aural detour: via police powers to curb noisy protest or through discriminating regimes and modalities of listening that classify and partition rage into "good" and "bad." Black rage is the focus, though not the exclusive concern, in this chapter because race as an exclusionary system predicated on a colonialist and patriarchal mission of "civilization" is always at work in the condemnation of incivility, whether it's explicitly on the face of it in any particular incident or not.

Bezos's quote-tweet condemned the Black professor precisely because she was someone "supposedly working to make the world better" (what else is a Black woman there to do in a university or civil society?) but, in his view, was failing to do this through her tweet. Other media outlets giving airtime and column inches to the professor's "side" of the debate have focused on the personal history that she referenced when responding to the original tweet, which was taken down by the platform on the grounds that it violated its rules: namely, that the state of which the British queen was the head had been responsible for the displacement and massacre of many of her relatives in the Biafran war and genocide. There were enduring consequences, especially for her mother, who was no stranger to the oppression of Trinidad's plantation colony from which she had emigrated. Both reactions reflect an apparent need to *justify* angry speech on the grounds either that it is fitting and proportionate to the injustice that provoked it or that it serves a laudable goal such as social change for the better. Rage that is unjustified in that it lacks proper measure, target, or purpose is frequently dismissed as excessive and counterproductive, primarily, so the reasoning goes, because it will go unheard. Rage—and especially Black rage—is figured as an excrescence to the European rational *logos*. It's too loud or too dissonant for the ears to parse. This is partly because, as Rei Terada has elucidated, European thought constructed that continent's populations and their descendants distributed around the world through imperialist "adventure" as uniquely capable of a relation to the other, whereas the intimacy and immediacy of the (especially African) other lacked the requisite distance or differentiation.[1] Rage is presented as alienating precisely because it seems to short circuit the processes of reasoning to get from o to 6o in the blink of an eye, admitting of little to no mediation in multiple senses of that word. It is an unsophisticated form of negation, less easily recuperated into *Aufhebung*. Moreover, rage seems to possess a subject more than it is an emotion in their possession. It is hence disquieting for theories of agency that turn on the will. Rage needs to be assigned a supervisor to *overhear* it (in the sense in which one oversees an unruly worker or slave).

A classic articulation of this bid to delimit angry expression by how it sounds to some ears is found in Audre Lorde's "The Uses of Anger." In that speech, she famously recounts how, at an academic conference at which she has spoken "out of a direct and particular anger," as she puts it, "a white woman comes up and says, 'Tell me how you feel but don't say it too harshly or *I cannot hear you*.' But is it my manner that keeps her from hearing, or the message that her life may change?"[2] Lorde goes on to insist that what a listener hears in her voice not be misheard as an expression of the moral authority of suffering (which might make it more palatable to white people since it is more readily amenable to emotional responses such as compassion) but as fury and anger. What Lorde's pithy question accentuates is that listening regulates just how harshly anger can be expressed before it is not heard at all, though one might also infer that it could just as well be insufficiently harsh to be heard *as* anger. Black rage seems condemned to meet the test of a Goldilocks's ears: not too hard, not too soft, but *just right*—necessarily hitting that sweet spot, pitch perfect, if it is to register as *just* or *right(eous)*. While the stereotyping of Black anger as irrational is especially pernicious, this racializing gesture is also applied to white protest: For example, if Extinction Rebellion protestors are righteous and articulate, an Irish folk singer still bemoaning British colonialism not so much. The latter is dismissed as "pining" for a long-lost era of "tribal antagonism" that offered a sense of "belonging" and "depth to his music"—music that now seemed bewildering to an audience mainly of tourists.[3]

There is a relation between tone and liberty such that the more one relies on taking liberty to advance a particular view, the less liberty one has to take a less measured tone. At one point in his discussion of freedom of thought and expression, Mill considers whether there ought to be restrictions on merely intemperate speech (short of "fighting words") and laments its unequal suppression, speculating that there would, conversely, be more justification to impose them on prevailing opinion than on minority or dissenting views, which "can only obtain a fair hearing by studied moderation of language and the most cautious avoidance of unnecessary offence, from which they hardly ever deviate even in a slightest degree without losing ground," in contrast with the "unmeasured vituperation" that does not deter people from listening to what in any event predominates.[4] This refinement of anger, moreover, depends on whom is being listened to as much as what is said or who is listening. Among today's clamors for free speech, including from quarters in which the anger of the most privileged increasingly threatens democratic liberties, white upper- or middle-class men continue to have the most latitude to shoot from the hip and miss the tonal bull's-eye, while women have to modulate far more, according to class and sexuality. Black folk above all, in differently gendered ways, are held to the highest standards of tuning in a system of temperament that has consistently branded them as irrational as Pythagoras's fifth hammer.

Only those who wouldn't incur the charge of incivility have the freedom for righteous incivility. That even polite white male republicans with modern received pronunciation are told in Britain today that "there's a time and a place" suggests that the scope for "speaking out of place," as David Palumbo-Liu calls it, is rapidly shrinking in a country whose ruling class has mustered no response to rage at colonialism or inequality besides nationalist delusion and hyperventilating exploitation.[5] And while American ears were pricked up by the furious sounds of crowds of Black Lives Matter protestors, drawn by their physiological energy, few tuned in (or at least not soon enough) to the quiet racist rage smoldering and burning holes through judicial and bureaucratic systems of government. In spring 2022 the UK government pushed through legislation (against the better judgment of the Lords) to give police powers to curb protest, even a single demonstrator, if they deemed the noise generated to cause serious disruption not only to essential services but also the timely circulation of capital or to result in not only harassment or intimidation of persons of reasonable firmness with the characteristics of persons likely to be in the vicinity but also alarm or distress to such persons.[6] A Home Office document aimed at dispelling "common misconception," which was mocked for telling police to take double-glazing into account, argued the new law wasn't incompatible with the government's much trumpeted commitments to free speech because police would be assessing the *level* and not the *content* of noise, seemingly unaware that they had quite literally passed a tone-policing law with all the discriminatory ramifications of that concept.[7] Noisy embodied rage will always be incommensurate with the structural violence of the state, masses on the streets with PA systems still on too human a scale to take the measure of it, yet disproportionately noisy and intense to its calm, calculating prosecution.

Lorde's analysis, while lucidly exposing this intersectional tuning, only hints at this incommensurability of Black rage— and in particular of its tone to its content—that motivates and unsettles its position in mappings of free expression, throwing an entire system's calibration off-key. For her, women's anger can be a source of transformational energy, though that requires precise articulation, which in turn demands that "we listen to the content of what is said with at least as much intensity as we defend ourselves from the manner of saying."[8] The relation between raging and listening, then, is not simply a zero-sum game, as suggested by the initial scene in which too much angry sound threatens to push out or overpower listening altogether. Rather, anger needs and inspires a certain modality of listening: intense, and specifically no less intense that the ear protection we construct to shield ourselves from anger's affective overload, its apostrophic demand on us that can be resisted only by turning our bodies away (human hearing is directional, and humans can't turn our ears like a cat or a wolf) or by holding one's ground while putting one's fingers in one's ears. In short, Black rage gets a hearing only when one stops fearing that hearing too much beating on one's eardrums will perforate them. The point is not to advocate enduring sonic violence in the name of liberation or denying someone the possibility of refusing to hear but that this perforation disrupts the violence of metaphysics' self-enclosure, figured as a voice-ear circuit that is "deaf" to difference from outside, as Jacques Derrida suggests in "Tympan" and has thus determined the rights to be heard and to refuse to hear in advance.[9] In this regard, there is an affinity between deconstruction and Black studies in their desire to pierce self-reproducing exclusionary institutions without reveling in the famed lack of earlids as if there were no narrowing of the aural passage to filter out resistance from hegemonic power. While thinkers such as Rancière or Nancy (who, not coincidentally, seek to revive liberal-humanist political concepts) illustrate the danger of boundaries returning in appeals to unrestricted democratization, in the economy of Derridean deconstruction the unconditional is qualified by the conditional and the conditioned. This resulting percussive syncopation of rage (part unleashed, part held back) also means, as I'll suggest by the end of the chapter, taking inspiration from another detail in Lorde's speech, that we must reframe our notions of anger away from that of a single—unconditional—knock-out blow.

We live in an age of anger, so the story goes. On both sides of the Atlantic, citizenries are torn apart by increasingly furious and vengeful polarization. If rage is all the rage, it makes good (liberal) sense to figure out which or whose anger to listen to and to what degree. That calls for a more refined and discerning aural apparatus to distinguish, amid the cacophony of rage, between the justified anger at racial injustice of Black Lives Matter and the nativist fury inflamed by the neo-Nazi's narcissistic injury, between the survivor of decades-long domestic violence who finally snapped and the entitled rapist indignant at being brought up short. Such listening cannot simply be reactive or on the receiving end of anger but operates, even if rarely credited explicitly, as the critical tool by which the volume of anger is dialed up and down in the political mix. Arguing that the rise of global Trumpism can be explained by what they dub "angrynomics," thereby suturing culture to political economy and slight to perceptions of inequality, economists Eric Lonergan and Mark Blyth find themselves contending with issues of listening in their conversational book. Anger, they argue in a reversal of the model I have just set out whereby listening regulates anger, is useful because, in a chaotic sociopolitical landscape, it points policymakers to what to listen to, how to respond, and to what ends so as to fix an economy that isn't working for the many. On a point of disagreement between them about the extent and impact of increasing inequality, Blyth observes that the economic analysis matters because if the righteous anger for which Lonergan wants to listen were to be misguided, as he suggests, that ought to change what one listens for.[10]

Ultimately, though, the authors of *Angrynomics* are most comfortable—as with many philosophers of anger before them—when it's clear to whom they should listen and who is allowed to be angry. Such clarity depends on competency in parsing the *legitimacy* of anger. While they argue that the ruling classes should be forced to listen to the moral outrage of those who have been ignored, they are eager to distinguish anger worthy of our ears from an unmerited tribal anger often stoked by the manipulation of politicians and the media for electoral gain and which they associate with violent football fans and white nationalists. The former is the anger of righteousness that seeks to right a wrong, the latter a primitive emotion without moral compass that wants to dominate. One is constructive in looking for change, the other out to have revenge against, even destroy, an outgroup on whom the blame can be pinned. What Lonergan in interviews has called the "anger of angels" can be explained and makes sense, while the "anger of devils," by contrast, is often vague and incoherent. While sympathetic to their political position, I detect a strong whiff of Platonic moralism here which, despite their manifest support for democracy, remains suspicious of disorderly emotion and tends to reproduce racializing stereotypes of "uncivilized" anger and of a lack of relation to difference.

"The challenge for politics today," Lonergan and Blyth say with seemingly unshaken confidence, "is to listen carefully to, and redress, the legitimate anger of moral outrage while exposing and not inciting, the violent anger of tribes."[11] Borrowing the language of legitimate grievances, they can only sustain the clear distinction by keeping apart the question of ethical norm violations from exclusionary mechanisms for forging collective identities, without recognizing their historical entanglement. Lonergan's archetype of tribal anger is nationalism, especially when it turns into terrorism (his chief example being the IRA), but, regardless of one's evaluation of Irish political history, his analysis is too brittle to be able to evaluate differently those situations in which liberation or separatist movements have adopted national or nationalist framings as a means of channeling energy and building resistance against a dominant and repressive nation-state nationalism, typically of an imperialist form, as Sivamohan Valluvan argues (his first example being the Irish resisting British supremacy).[12] Again, I cite this example not to take "sides" or suggest one pair of Irish yet British-educated ears is more finely attuned to injustice than another. The test of liberatory nationalisms will be whether those negational energies are later ossified into a regime that secures its integrity by turning instead against internal racialized communities, which might also include the (white) allegedly "undeserving" poor. In other words, it will hinge on whether its conceptions of freedom are predicated upon an exclusionary construction of sovereignty. My concern in this chapter, however, is with whether we should depend *on our ears* to test the legitimacy of, and therefore to regulate, angry expression and whether such listening itself rests upon not only the vantage point of the listener but also a metaphysical conception of a sovereign listening or speaking subject.

Lonergan and Blyth argue that their sharp distinction does not necessitate blocking out the sound of tribal anger altogether but rather exposing it as the product of attempts to exploit the justified anger and anxiety that stem from economic micro-stressors and insecurity so that they might be contained, rather than fueled, and the underlying drivers addressed. Before turning to the specific ways in which listening acts as an anger filter to classify and partition its acceptable expression, I want to pause to analyze this metaphorics of containment and the way in which it binds together rage and listening. While it is, of course, perfectly possible to stew quietly in one's own anger or to rage into a pillow or a storm unheard, anger is importantly regarded as a social emotion and, for the most part, therefore implicates a listener (which might even be the minimal therapeutic idea that the angry person should listen to their own feelings and manifestations of anger). It strives to be heard and especially for the kind of listening that affords uptake and understanding.

Rage is also connected with aurality in that a lack of listening—a feeling of going unheard—is itself a spur to anger, which is further compounded when the expression of that anger and, hence, its legitimacy is denied through silencing of one kind or another. It is this double injury that Jean-François Lyotard articulates with his notion of the *différend*, whereby the original damage is compounded by the fact that it cannot be brought to the attention of or recognized by others.[13] As Lyotard teases out, an injured party is put in a double bind by the aporias of a listening that either gives no credibility to the testimony whatsoever or that surmises that a wrong that is audible is not so outrageous for that very fact. The assumption here is that listening has always already softened the blow. If one is heard (out) because the anger is justified by the wrong, one is then immediately denied the possibility of remaining angry, since the wrong has now been heard. The risk of going unheard, of a lack of testimonial credibility or of due weight, is both a source of anger in itself and a motivation for angry expression in a bid to impress the testimony upon the ears of anyone who will listen. And yet, as Lorde observes, if that anger, even if justified by a wrong, should appear out of proportion to that wrong—because it is calibrated, furthermore, to the measure of the risk of going unheard, in other words, to the double penalty of both the wrong and the damage of its mishearing—then anger will always be in excess of the listening it demands. Hence bell hooks will wonder what hope there is for multiracial collectivity "if white people remain unable to hear black rage, if it is the sound of that rage which must always remain repressed, contained, trapped in the realm of the unspeakable."[14]

The worry about what might be described as a sadomasochistic bond implicitly informs philosophical counsel against the expression of anger (or advises it only in strictly limited circumstances or degrees). Before turning to those influential skeptical arguments, I want to put some pressure on the nature of this codependency and the underlying assumptions it makes about both anger and listening. For Sue J. Kim, who approaches anger from the perspective of cultural studies, arguing for a more collective and structural theory than the individualized accounts typical of moral philosophy or cognitive psychology, Lorde retains a normative framework, albeit one in which Black rage registers and protests against the violation of *group* norms of ethics, justice, and human rights.[15] On this view, anger's value lies in the clarifying social analyses that undergird it and hence in its ability to educate and thereby effect change. Kim cites hooks on the need "to tap collective black rage [to] move it beyond fruitless scapegoating of any group, linking it instead to a passion for freedom and justice that illuminates."[16] In this metaphor of tapping, reflecting a quasi-hydraulic concept of emotion, listening serves to lift the repression, to liberate anger.

It is not immediately self-evident why listening should be especially suited to such a task when we also speak of the invisibility of the oppressed and their suffering. Sonali Chakravati, writing about the role of listening to rage in truth and reconciliation processes, turns to a surprising source to locate an aural turn. She notices that it is at those moments when Adam Smith deviates from his Stoic picture of sympathy as restrained, moderated, and oriented toward self-cultivation and government that his habitual visual metaphors, underscoring emotional detachment and spectatorship, are displaced by aural ones of voice and pitch. As in Plato's critique of democracy, sound is associated with an excess or incommensurability of feeling. Insofar as anger is even more cacophonous and alienating than other shows of emotion, including the wailing of lamentation that he bemoans as symptomatic of an ungovernable (and feminized) soul, it prompts fear and aversion. This is what makes it harder to retain the cool impartiality of the eye. This analysis, however, repeats the stereotypical binary oppositions of the now clichéd audio-visual litany: vision takes place at a distance, while aurality is associated with proximity and immediacy; the eye stands for individual reasons, while the ear is collective; and so on. Yet Smith's shift to sonic metaphors serves as a "linchpin" for Chakravarti's theory. An ethics of listening is more intimate and responsive and hence is better suited than seeing to discern the gradations and varieties of anger. It is also more attentive to the particular. Furthermore, rather than evaluating proportionality, aurality is presumed to promote participation, bonding, and the bridging of emotion and action.

Smith's theory of anger, though, is not straightforwardly mimetic. Unlike grief or joy, which he thinks inspires the same emotions in the listener (or at least disposes them to imagine those feelings), anger provokes fear, which is an obstacle to sympathy. This is especially so when it is "not 'toned down to a pitch' where it can be more easily heard."[17] Listening, then, is like a mixing desk that does not blend all the different voices into a consonant harmony but retains a degree of agonism, at the same time allowing the listener to lower the volume of their own inner voice to put the other's voice in the foreground of the mix. If reconciliation processes require sufficient trust to take the edge off the performance of vulnerability, listening's "presumptive generosity" to the kinetic, intense aspect of anger has the capacity to "set a new tone" and is braced for the "unpredictability, excessiveness, and physicality of testimony," as well as attuned to the unsaid in speech.[18]

One of the reasons for the entanglement of rage and listening is the extent to which therapeutic frameworks promote an ideal of cathartic discharge, of which empathetic listening is held to be an efficacious instrument. For Sam Binkley, the neoliberal-managerialist co-option of this psychologization of (out)rage and struggles against racism has bound the couple in "an unholy contract."[19] In part this is because listening is held to alleviate the alienation and double injury of the *différend* or testimonial injustice analyzed earlier, to relieve the pressures of the op-, sup-, and re-pressions variously at work to make the blood boil, and as such to serve as a kind of release valve to let off the steam. But it is also crucially to subl(im)ate it into something more productive or contain it so as to return dangerous emotions to the speaker "defused" or, as other analysts might say, "contained." What makes psychoanalytical listening distinctive and potent, though, is that it amplifies "emotional undertones," functioning as a "microphone" of the unconscious in the words of Theodore Reik.[20] On the one hand, the psychologization of rage justified the criminalization of Blackness and excesses of the carceral state through stigmatization of Black emotionality or "animatedness." On the other hand, it underwrote a post-Fordist process of pressing listening into the service of managerial containment, allowing capital to extend into one of a number of affective spheres, evading its capture via autonomous creativity or via battering its gates in the fight against racial and colonial oppression. Within this framework the real pay-off, however, has been listening's capacity to lift the lid off the white psyche, to expose unconscious bias, to reveal the truth of whiteness, and to offer insight and clarity, while at the same time mobilizing empathetic responsiveness to impose a modicum of order upon pathologized feeling. The valorization of listening in management studies, the self-help industry, and the political sphere (among centrist elites convinced the key to their power lay in listening tours and focus groups) was all about blunting the force of negative emotions like anger that threatened the orderly transfer and sharing of power within the establishment. And when universities promote top-down visions for decolonizing curricula or fossil-fuel companies wax lyrical about corporate social responsibility, the tapped rage of people of color serves to demystify whiteness so as to preserve its innocence in the guise of ignorance. Listening becomes, in Binkley's turn of phrase, "the philosopher's stone of post-racist white subjectivity, sought after for its alchemical properties"—or the alibi of the racial contract at the heart of social-contract theory.[21]

Chakravarti's notion of listening, however, strives for something else. For her, confrontational anger is not looking for uptake or recognition but seeks to expose the limits of the political system, including the impossibility of complete resolution or repair in the wake of violence and, I would suggest, the limitations of a neoliberal listening apparatus designed as it is to cathect negative feelings toward its own ends by ordaining them for some project of the self on the part of speaker or listener. Without listening, she argues, the expression of anger remains merely cathartic or monologic, and unconnected to justice. Listening, on this definition, isn't restricted to a power of relief but is precisely what enables catharsis to transform into a vehicle for justice because it promotes trust. It redirects libidinal energy. And yet Chakravarti rejects both Marxist fears that rage burns up energy for purposeful collective action and the liberal-democratic model of delineating that condemns any expression that smacks of a narcissistic anger that "hears only itself" while exculpating rage that becomes a catalyst for social movements. "Righteous" anger, then, is defined by having a goal outside itself, which thereby purifies anger. Like Agnes Callard, Chakravarti has greater tolerance for the messiness of an emotion that resists such parsing.[22] And yet the link to listening remains strong. The restorative justice approach sees more intrinsic value in anger than the skeptical or therapeutic traditions, though, precisely because of its relational and conversational focus. Anger has potential political benefits because it makes high demands of an audience's listening skills and thereby holds open the possibility for a more agonistic politics, making democracy more robust than a consensual model. Anger is still absolved by listening, pardoned because its fruit might, through those aural labors, just be a more desirable political community.

Among anger skeptics listening is rarely thematized extensively, although this tradition typically derives its evaluations and disapprobations from the *hearing* that rage gets or doesn't. Martha Nussbaum, who famously and contentiously argues that retribution is conceptually inherent to anger, attributes its conversion into something more productive to a certain aural capacity. When Athena convinces the Furies to transition to the project of democracy, they must undergo a series of changes, including exchanging retributive urges for benevolent sentiments and refraining from stirring up trouble, but "perhaps most fundamentally transformative of all," remarks Nussbaum, "they must listen to the voice of persuasion."[23] This she sees as a sign of an "inner reorientation" that goes to the heart of personality. Nussbaum also recognizes the failure to listen, or an insistence on speaking while refusing to listen, as a source of social discord and as something that provokes or compounds anger. Listening figures as a solution when it is practiced by angry speakers themselves, rather than their audiences, so if listening assuages anger, it is not so much that anger must be listened to than that anger must learn to listen (to other voices). Not only in the presence of listening but, moreover, in cultivating practices of learning to listen, rage is to transmute into an engine of democratic deliberation.

The capacity to listen *in* anger (not so much *to* anger) is thus what, in Nussbaum's book, separates a productive transitional anger (which is no longer anger at all but already compassionate hope for social betterment and advocacy for social reform or rehabilitation) from a futile infantile rage (which cannot get beyond nursing its own aggrieved powerlessness and which is self-defeating because it clouds good judgment). The desire for revenge, she maintains, has no use for changing the future, for it only offers an illusion of control and freedom, whereas the recognition of wrong, in itself, can be socially and politically productive. Martin Luther King is the paradigm, for her, of anger purified of its retributive fantasy, his critique of Malcolm X understood as moral indictment rather than a disagreement over tactics.

Skeptics such as Nussbaum and Owen Flanagan are eager to displace anger in favor of emotions more palatable to the listener, confirming Lorde's suspicion that in tone policing the listening gets to dictate the terms on which the expression is heard. "In anger policing," writes Myisha Cherry, "anger is not only always inappropriate but also always disproportionate. Anger, for the evaluator, is always felt and thus evaluated as too intense, too much, and too loud that it blocks the evaluator from hearing anything the angry has to say."[24] Even if not all criticism of anger seeks to police, Cherry rejects the tendency of listeners insensitive to others' experiences to be more concerned with how the anger makes the listener feel than with the cause of the anger, for it often distracts from that lack of interest or will to understand or sympathize. This implication, moreover, that the angry person is too loud or too intense for the listener's eardrums only amplifies the speaker's anger at not being heard, or perhaps, more precisely, at being *over-heard* as if intensely surveilled and—borrowing the double sense of *overlooked*—as if what they have to say and the reason for their anger were passed over in favor of hearing too much in the manner of their speaking. Céline Leboeuf makes the sharp observation, following Fanon's phenomenology of the anger of the colonized, that such rage has value in that it can defend against internalizing the white colonizer's point of view or listening and against the destabilizing, potentially silencing effect of suddenly hearing oneself speak as if one were over(-)hearing oneself instead of the usual transparency of the mouth-ear circuit.[25] The result is that too much hearing, too much aural attunement to the modulation and tone of expression, leads to no more hearing, the ear exhausted. But one might also, thinking of Sianne Ngai's analysis of how ugly feelings are undecidable between subjective and objective, put some pressure on the clear-cut distinction between the speaker and the audience, and on their sovereign enclosed circuits of listening.

Complicating the story of auto-affection has significant ramifications for the evaluation of anger. Several feminists of color concede the need to distinguish justifiable anger. Even while countering the instrumental argument against counterproductivity, Amia Srinivasan, nonetheless, maintains that there is an intrinsic reason for anger only when it is fitting or apt.[26] Cherry, too, identifying as a "variation artist," thinks it is worth distinguishing between different types of anger, more or less worthy of our approval or opprobrium if not exactly, therefore, more or less audible, on the basis of their target, action tendency, and aim.[27] Rather than straightforwardly adopt metaphysical principles as yardsticks for evaluating rage, Cherry presents a series of cameos of raging speakers. The "rogue rage" of, for example, a neo-Nazi is indiscriminate and nihilistic, misses its target in lashing out at everyone, and has no interest in resolution. "Wipe rage" wants to eliminate the scapegoated other and is premised on a zero-sum game of them or us—hence its prevalence in white nativism. If these are obvious candidates for our condemnation, the next two types require more careful parsing because they readily find expression in the mouths of the colonial subjects who envy their colonizers, the Indigenous people who want retribution against all white settlers, or the Black men who ascend to positions of power. In common with a number of authors (except, notably, Callard), Cherry is suspicious of ressentiment rage, which envies the (racial) other in a position of power, is reactive, and wants revenge. Likewise, the narcissistic rage named by bell hooks that belongs to elites, including those of color, is status oriented. Instead of humiliating the other, they think they deserve better treatment, but this is rooted in egocentric exceptionalism ("how dare you treat *me* like this!"), not anger at systemic injustice and the suffering of others.

Cherry singles out for advocacy what she calls Lordean rage. Echoing some of the spirit of the skeptical tradition, Lordean rage, even though not judged on the basis of its effects, earns its regard because its action tendency is to use it for energy. It is itself transformative, however, rather than transitional in that it doesn't need to give way to other emotions to effect the change at which it aims. Unlike an ideal type, Lordean rage is, moreover, attainable rather than raised up on an impossibly high pedestal. This kind of rage is not necessarily noble; while it requires some moral sensitivity and imagination, it doesn't demand excellence. It can go wrong if one, for example, becomes fixated at the expense of caring for others or oneself. It's not exclusive: it admits of other cognitive and affective responses alongside rage, thereby also making room for diversity of tactics in the struggle against racism. It can, following Brittney Cooper, be "eloquent" without being "elegant," clear in its demands without being respectable.[28] Lordean rage aims at changing the beliefs, values, and policies that sustain systems of oppression, such as white supremacy, but not as the destruction of the other. Rather, in contradistinction to Lonergan and Blyth's tribal anger, it is radically inclusive, hitching the fate of one's freedom to that of the other. Cherry echoes Lorde: "I am not free while [any] other is unfree."[29]

If these sound like a lot of conditions on anger, perhaps they are. Elsewhere Cherry suggests that, since there are a number of obstacles to evaluating the political anger of others, in the end we'd be better off listening to them instead of judging their anger.[30] If the difficulties of empathizing with anger without knowing the cause, sympathy gaps with those less proximate, tone policing, and gaslighting make it next to impossible accurately to assess the worthiness of another's anger in the time typically taken to judge, it seems unreasonable to ask the oppressed to navigate epistemic and affective terrains where their anger may be more or less intelligible. Given this, one might deduce that another kind of listening is also called for: namely, attunement to the structural stereotyping of emotion and affect or, otherwise put, to the habitual and structural ways of listening to others in a society. This would entail something like over-hearing hearing, submitting the prevailing norms and distributions of audibility to the same degree of intense scrutiny that silences the marginalized. This would be repurposing philosophy or reviving its critical function to listen with attentiveness and circumspection to how power is wielded—rather than prosecuting an analytic of truth, veracity, or normativity, sounding the alarm bells of errant soundings. Otherwise put, this would require liberating listening—and democracy with it—from a dialectic of consonance and dissonance, and instead recognizing that the sonic field is much more differentiated and self-differentiating.

Leboeuf cautions against dismissing all but untainted anger chiefly because it can foster a sense of self-determined Black agency in the face of the racial schema woven and imposed by the white ear.[31] Callard is even more suspicious of the urge to purify, accusing Stoic skeptics fearful of anger's vengefulness and sentimentalists who reclaim anger for its capacity to sensitize people to injustice of engaging in a pseudo-debate insofar as the second camp only mount this defense provided its less palatable elements are shorn off. They want "all of the virtues and none of the vices of anger."[32] In short, this is a fantasy of freedom—of freeing anger from everything that might make it unfree. But this is the freedom of a sovereign subject, master of their will, in control of their emotions, free to determine their actions, and their acts well intentioned. That those intentions might go astray is a thought too far for a liberalism embattled by too many other menaces and the fallout of its own broken promises.

Both arguments against resentment and limited defenses tend to worry about power, agency, and capacity. The chief argument against an expression of rage tainted by resentment is that it ties the speaker to an experience of powerlessness, which, in Miguel de Beistegui's argument, leaves one "locked in" to passivity, one's thinking "chained in" to the question of blame and retribution.[33] This is the opposite of the expansive notion of critical capacity or "faculty" that he develops as a counterweight to noetic, pre-epistemic vices that impede thought as a condition for knowledge, such as spite, superstition, and stupidity. And yet it remains unclear why it would be necessary for a critique of power to take the form of an "I can," of a performativity or sovereign power. As such, this proposal appears to fall short of the critical ambitions that he has for philosophy in that it leaves intact the structure of possibilization, of a potential that gives itself to itself undergirding the ideology of power. Its purchase on power is less than it might be in that it does not subject its organizing fiction to scrutiny, which would expose the errancy that affects any power or faculty from the outset. By castigating resentment for its attachment to the unfreedom of the powerless, this analysis leaves freedom bound to the notion of sovereign performative power and denies it the freedom to find other freedoms—precisely those that might arise from resentment at facing a dialectical choice between potential and impotential that leaves no room for the resistant, the contingent, the impossible internal to all power.

Rage is valuable precisely because it taps into that impossibility of the possible without relieving it. Pondering what this *tapping* might entail also means undoing the position of a listener who says, "I can hear your rage, I am capable of listening to it," undoing that vantage point that can synthesize, assess, survey, and surveil the sonic field. When Lorde speaks of the need "to tap into that anger as a source of empowerment," she offers an unwitting clue to other modalities of freedom and power when she says that this entails that one "listen to its rhythms."[34] What if we were to take this tap in another sense, not an extractivist or therapeutic one, but of an instrument that both overhears (like a wiretap) and does so by gentle rhythmic percussion (like auscultation)? Auscultation doesn't just listen to or even from a single point. It over-punctuates, dividing the points it taps. Peter Szendy in fact suggests that not only does auscultation listen for multiple signs in at one point; it also resembles "the discriminating faculty that we call echolocation, which, in both animals and humans, resides in the gap between the two tympana."[35] Every tap, if I put it like this, is always already a double tap, which pinpoints the object of listening via an interaural difference. Raging or listening to rage need not be understood through the lens of an agency, capacity, power, or even a concept looking to draw up its frontier. If rage and listening are both frontier concepts—on the frontier (of civilization, reason, certainty, empire) and overtaking it so as to take over what lies beyond—they therefore make the very notion of a frontier or limit (to freedom of expression, or anything else) tremble. The freedom of expression to cross a line (of civility, tone, volume) is better understood as a matter of binaural (or polyaural) echolocation since the possibility of securing a single vantage point from which to adjudicate the limit is put in question by cases of raging or otherwise excessive expression. In this way the differantial and conditional pluralization of the limit in deconstruction makes common purpose not with liberal multiculturalism but with forms of thought that challenge the ongoing persistence of empire, patriarchy, and the afterlives of slavery.

Compassion is one potential alternative to ressentiment in the face of injustice, suffering, and anger but which also entails that one make positive or negative judgments on, and take the measure of, others' suffering. Writing about this emotion of compassion, Lauren Berlant sharply observes how neoliberalism converts social indignities into the grounds for the entrepreneurial project of the self who pulls themself up by the bootstraps, making injustice and inequality "a problem of will and ingenuity."[36] But in individualizing or localizing compassion and amelioration away from the state, it arguably forms less the solidarity of the powerless than "the apex of affective agency" and the height of condescension.[37] And yet there is an overwhelming desire to purify compassion of any of its complicated dynamics, including duty or what might sometimes be reluctance, withholding, or aversion, to provide reassurance that it is straightforwardly well intentioned.

Srinivasan suggests that more than a moral judgment, rage might be likened to a pre-epistemic "aesthetic appreciation" of injustice, but this does not immediately resolve the problem of the communicability of the exemplarily singular, as the transcendental aesthetic reveals.[38] Lyotard's reading of Kant's *sensus communis* borrows a raft of musical metaphors to describe aesthetic judgment not as social consensus but as the auto-affection of the subject as an "interior music" or "intimacy of sounds," or, more precisely, "the division of the subject as a division ac(c/h)orded for one moment, called together in convocation," as if it were the effect of an apostrophizing interpellation from the other (in me).[39] It is perhaps no coincidence that Berlant, too, invokes an expressly aural metaphor when they conclude their reflections by quoting a famous passage in George Eliot's *Middlemarch* that characterizes common suffering as the scarcely audible sounds of nature and the chaotic, unknowable inner world of the other as "that roar which lies on the other side of silence." J. Hillis Miller hears in the passage the ruin of the self as a force or power to create fictional coherence, here shipwrecked on the cacophonous feeling of ordinary human life.[40] The only protection, Eliot says, is that great enemy of a particular species of freedom of expression proper to the university—the "wadding" of stupidity.

5

Lies, Bullshit, and Sophistry

Vicious Universities

In February 2022 I was asked to comment on a response to the consultation on a proposed Bill of Rights in the UK whose focus was specifically on protections for academic freedom. The most challenging issues had to do with the *standards* required of academic expression, and yet given that academics are accorded, by both the judiciary and certain segments of the public, a very high degree of authority as watchdogs in a democratic society, the hearing they receive has a tremendous bearing on the arguments in this book. The issue of standards qualifying academic expression is made all the more complex because of the atypical character of, and the ambivalence academics often feel toward, their professional employment status. This status means that they are held to standards insofar as they are employees *and* insofar as they are academics (researchers, educators, public intellectuals, informed citizens) with all the contradictions between those demands. The American Association of University Professors' (AAUP) 1915 *Declaration of Principles on Academic Freedom and Academic Tenure* even made the dubious—and I would argue depoliticizing—claim that, in fact, professors are not employees at all. One of the potential issues, if arguably a tactical benefit, of relying on the First Amendment or with the recent Higher Education (Freedom of Speech) Act 2023 in the UK, which assigns jurisdiction to the (very expensive) High Court, is that it takes the exercise of academic freedom of expression out of the arena of an employment dispute, as if it were (solely) a matter of universal human rights. Even though the Strasbourg jurisprudence is sensitive to minoritarian rights, the increase in reactionary appeals to rights (from white supremacists, for example) drives academic freedom headlong into the "problem of the rights line" identified by W. E. B. Du Bois. Moreover, the question of standards and the issues of listening they provoke cannot be extricated from the material conditions of exploitation and oppression into a sphere of transhistorical normativity.

The UK Bill of Rights Bill, which frankly fell too far short of drafting standards so as effectively to achieve its putative goal of restricting the influence of the European Court of Human Rights (ECtHR) in Strasbourg, was subsequently withdrawn in its current form by Liz Truss, as one of her first (and least disastrous) acts as prime minister after the ousting of Boris Johnson, though withdrawal from the Convention has remained attractive to the right of the Conservative Party. The issue of specifically *academic* expression, however, remains of legislative concern on both sides of the Atlantic, as well as of broader policy concern for the EU, which must contend with how the issue manifests itself differently in different kinds of regime, from Turkey and Hungary to Germany and France. The UK Higher Education (Freedom of Speech) Act has eventually ended up on the statute books, but the consultation response on which I offered feedback concerning standards still remains of the utmost relevance and was never addressed in amendments to the Bill. The legislation and regulatory regime it creates, which are far more concerned with free speech on campus, will do next to nothing to protect academic freedom in its specificity. I was among those urging more definitional precision on the face of the Bill during its passage through Parliament and, failing that, in a voluntary code adopted by the sector. These concerns persist, especially if the European Convention of Human Rights (ECHR) were ever to be thrown in the bin and the link to Strasbourg severed entirely. As I polished off the manuscript for this book, this folly was being bandied around again with renewed vigor as an election campaign platform, with renewed attacks on "politicized" European judges who would block the deportation of asylum seekers to Rwanda, even though the highest domestic courts found against the government on the basis of other international law principles.

Meanwhile over the past few years in the United States, alongside an ongoing flow of high-profile cases of individual academics disciplined or dismissed over contentious expression, a number of state legislatures, emboldened by a resurgence of Republican reaction, have introduced bills aiming to clamp down on the teaching, in both secondary and higher education, of what Trump and Republican lawyers have dubbed "divisive concepts" on the grounds that they may induce feelings of guilt, shame, anguish, or psychological distress. While some of the clauses in the proposed provisions target conduct already reasonably prohibited by anti-discrimination law, others would have the effect of curbing advocacy for affirmative action (which has only recently been struck down as "unconstitutional" by the U.S. Supreme Court), even where this reflected the institution's own policies or teaching in a critical way about the system of race, the concept of white supremacy, or the imbrication of certain notions, such as meritocracy, in colonialist ideology. One tactic adopted by the right in both the United States and the UK has been to erode the distinction between freedom of expression and academic freedom so as, in seeming to widen the scope of the former on campuses, to regulate more closely the criticality held to be proper to the latter. Key to understanding the current state of affairs and to navigating this often highly contentious terrain is therefore to scrutinize the ways in which academic freedom has been defined in relation to "simple" or "ordinary" free speech.

Albeit in different ways, the conventional way of delimiting academic freedom has been to point to the professional nature of the right—in other words, that the special protection arises in some way from the professional standing or employment relationship of academics. While some have seen this as a privilege to be justified or deployed responsibly, others have argued for an intrinsic relationship that, conversely, enables privilege of all forms to be challenged. On one side of the debate, Thomas Docherty echoes arguments developed over the course of the twentieth century in the United States when he describes academic freedom as "the very founding condition of the possibility of an academic doing her or his job at all."[1] More than a "necessity" or "prerequisite" for individual academics, it is what makes institutions socially responsible and as such it is also "the founding condition of the very possibility of social freedom." Attacks on academic freedom are therefore attacks on popular democracy and justice. I shall return to these justifications of academic freedom as a public good, but it is the distinctively *professional* character of this species of freedom of expression that has posed particular challenges for defining its scope.

This professional definition of academic freedom invites two notable categories of restriction on academic freedom of expression (AFOE). (I use this term to distinguish the expression component of a much broader concept of academic freedom that includes institutional autonomy as a necessary though not sufficient condition for a set of free-speech and other individual rights accorded to academics with particular weight and limits.) The first of these categories of restriction arises from the employment relationship, which is perhaps the most significant brake on AFOE. The Strasbourg Court has held that academics are in the unique position of being able to criticize the institution or system in which one works even, as the jurisprudence of the ECtHR avers, where that may have the effect of bringing the institution into disrepute.[2] Such criticism will also necessarily come up against contractual terms, including the implied mutual obligation of trust and confidence between employer and employee, as it does for all employees. Expression calculated or likely to destroy that relationship without proper cause may well fall outside the scope of legal protection, but the academic setting, with its distinctive value of academic freedom, will be crucial for determining, on the facts, what is reasonable, as will the target which, as a public institution, might reasonably expect to be subject to critical scrutiny and robust disapproval in ways that individuals would not, especially when the issues are of public interest. As I've remarked with a wry smile to the vice-chancellor at my former institution, where I led the work on academic freedom, there's typically sufficient clear water between substantiable criticism of action taken in his official capacity and my mouthing off on Twitter that "Stuart is a total [beep] and an utter [beep] [beep]," without ever having raised my complaint within university governance structures.

In cases concerning institutional and third-party reputational interests, as well as cases of potential negative stereotyping, Strasbourg jurisprudence has identified a number of features that suggest AFOE will prevail. These broadly fall into two categories: the quality of what is said and the manner in which it is said. Reputational interest, for example, is likely to be trumped where there is sufficient factual basis for the criticism and the academic has acquitted themself of an obligation to back up their claims with evidence, even where the criticism turns out not to be true: in other words, demonstrating one had sufficient reasons to believe it to be true. The Court has also considered the degree of hyperbole warranted, noting in the same case that the academic "did not resort to offensive and intemperate language and did not go beyond the generally acceptable degree of exaggeration."[3] Without using the lexicon typical in the United States—for example, in the case of Steven Salaita, who was fired by the University of Illinois for tweets deemed "uncivil"—the Strasbourg Court has taken a view that certain forms of expression protected in the public domain may cross a line in the workplace to the extent that they erode mutual trust: "The requirement to act in good faith does not imply an absolute duty of loyalty towards the employer or a duty of discretion to the point of subjecting the worker to the employer's interest [but] an attack on the respectability of individuals by using grossly insulting or offensive expressions in the professional environment is, on account of its disruptive effects, a particularly serious form of misconduct capable of justifying severe sanctions."[4] The context and reasoning in this case made it clear that gratuitous ad hominem attacks in the context of employment are likely to exceed the freedom to express ideas that "offend, shock, or disturb," as a well-known and oft-cited legal formulation has it.[5]

However, that finding was not in the context of *academic* employment, in which the right to criticize the institution in which one works is an intrinsic part of the mutual expectations and of academic self-governance. In fact, the Court carefully distinguished the earlier case just quoted in a case certain to make any head of department or chair raise an eyebrow. Having been notified of the merger of his department with another, that this would lead to the abolition of his own position, and that he would be dismissed if he refused to comply, the applicant did what many in his position might do: He wrote a letter to the rector complaining of a lack of democracy and transparency in the dean's decision-making process and proposing a series of governance reforms for consideration at the upcoming meeting of the University Senate. At the same time, he drew attention to allegations of institutional financial mismanagement, citing the findings of the State Audit Office. When the Senate upheld the dean's decision against the applicant's protestations, he wrote a further letter to the rector setting out a proposed settlement agreement and reserving his right to go public with the financial "illegalities" as well as allegations that the university had turned a blind eye to plagiarism among its staff due to nepotism. The head of the department was summarily dismissed for uncollegial and unethical conduct contrary to labor law—a decision upheld by the domestic courts. The majority on the ECtHR, however, did not accept the respondent's arguments that the email amounted to "blackmail," distinguishing ECHR Article 10 rights from whistleblowing cases in which the motives of the speaker are relevant, but this view was rejected by two judges in their dissenting opinion.

On the question of uncivil or insulting words, the applicant had perhaps gone further than an average department chair in highlighting personal moral failings of senior management (a devout Catholic was condemned as hypocritical for having children out of wedlock, another administrator accused of lying, and another of urging staff to break the law to aid her protégés). The majority thought that the letter to the rector had stopped short of divulging any private information harmful to the honor or dignity of those colleagues or to the institution as a whole, relying on the fact that when a national news agency published his views on allegations of financial mismanagement, they were not contested as untrue and hence defamatory, and they did not extend to personal barbs. Much may turn here on the fact that the academic pursued his complaint, however personally insulting the tone of his emails, via internal channels—something underscored by the Court. One might also wonder whether the fact that he was punching up in an academic environment could have been an important factor, in contrast with the distinguished nonacademic case in which the impugned cartoons posted on a notice board by trade unionists could be seen as punching sideways or even down at the representatives of a committee of nonsalaried delivery workers depicted and described as rolling over and frolicking like guard dogs "in return for a pat on the back by their master."[6]

Criticism of those perceived to have "sold out" those with whom they share experiences of exploitation or oppression, if not identical material interests, is especially contentious when it comes to targets of color, and it becomes necessary to draw a line between racial slurs that wouldn't be protected and scholarly analyses or concepts that would be. The conventional liberal-democratic position tends to make tone or civility the arbiter in such cases, but, as Steven Salaita has argued, civility is a "mechanism of plutocratic common sense."[7] In other words, as Arianne Shahvisi observes, extant notions of civility conceal and uphold operative power differentials, or at best are indifferent to them.[8] Part of this power is *epistemic*. Shahvisi holds the view that academics do enjoy a certain epistemic privilege on account of greater, sometimes overinflated credibility and also a certain "platform privilege" given their access to a wide range of audiences. If they are more likely than most to be given a hearing, they should therefore be required to exercise this privilege responsibly. One issue with appeals to civility is that tone and credibility are in the ears of the listener, and the majority of those listeners are already most empowered to control the distributions of audibility in the academy. The academy is, in this regard, little different from other public systems and institutions whose participation in structural oppression consists in burdening bodies and voices that deviate from norms with the presumption of disrespect or intemperance.

This weaponization of civility against the academic freedom

of minorities is embedded into norms of professional conduct: activists may yell in the streets, but intemperate tweets do not befit a professor. Mindful of such repressive tendencies and of the dogmatism inherent in rejections of *all* appeals to civility, Teresa Bejan aspires to reclaim seventeenth-century tolerationist postures of minimal civility—which might translate today into modes of listening that, through charity, tact, discretion, pragmatic keeping silent, or even simply attentive listening, would prevent affectively overwhelming disagreement having a chilling effect on debate and hold open the space for a shared sense or common ground.[9] In a different vein, Shahvisi seeks to reclaim and inject new meaning into an ameliorative concept of civility. Such civility would demand that academics use the epistemic advantage of their opportunity to be heard and believed to "counter-hegemonic" ends so as to "offset" testimonial injustice outside academia.[10] This is not only because it is *morally* right but because of its *epistemic* rewards, since in making space for voices that are usually silent, silenced, unheard, or disbelieved, it serves the interests of diversifying knowledge sources and of thereby reducing tendencies toward epistemic marginalization that shrink possibilities for truth acquisition. Angry or outraged speech could certainly qualify for Shavisi's definition of civility, which puts the epistemic mission of the university above implicit demands from the student-consumer, donor, or trustee that they not be made to feel uncomfortable on account of their privilege. This idea that learning may—or perhaps even *ought* to—provoke discomfort is a familiar argument among defenders of academic freedom, though arguably the line between intellectual discomfort and discrimination is being tested by right-wing proponents, and Shahvisi does not address contemporary demands for safety or distinctions between intellectual and dignity safety. In other respects Shahvisi adopts a fairly conventional liberal understanding of the professional standards expected of academics without asking in detail how those professional and disciplinary norms themselves reproduce the structures of oppression that she rightly highlights. The rest of this chapter is devoted to examining those standards and the epistemic arguments made for and against them. In particular it considers how academic freedom entails intellectual risk and courage for which no training can prepare us, and that this risk is deeply entangled with freedom of listening.

If collegial self-governance has traditionally been seen as an essential component of academic freedom and a condition for upholding individual rights of intramural and extramural expression, this has supported the idea that academic communities have the right to determine and regulate for themselves the standards to which they should hold their members. This capacity to self-determine academic standards is precisely what is being challenged by the CEO of private equity firm Apollo Global Management, who co-leads the Boards of Advisors at the University of Pennsylvania's Wharton School, in the wake of President Liz Magill's failure, when cornered at a congressional committee or, indeed, in the weeks beforehand, to articulate a nuanced, coherent defense of free speech on campus sensitive to racial and religious oppression against the backdrop of Israel's ongoing assaults on Palestinians in Gaza and a rise in both antisemitic and Islamophobic attacks in the United States. Institutional autonomy risks being another casualty of these circumstances, though such incidents also underscore Derrida's point that the self-determination of disciplines—or, more precisely, philosophy's privilege of self-determination in Kant's *Conflict of the Faculties*—is itself politically determined (by the state's withdrawal of its power to overhear).[11]

In spite of such attacks on academic self-governance, there's an implicit conception of the scholarly discipline as the liberal sovereign subject, which enjoys negative freedom from undue external interference. Given this, one might think campus conduct policies could reasonably be restricted to interfering only where expression becomes unlawful, though failure to explain why or reflect on the possible shortcomings of this approach is partly why the three university presidents came unstuck during the congressional hearing. This would include breaches of the criminal law that would, in any event, be excluded from First Amendment protection or by virtue of Article 17 in states signed up to the ECHR, as well as breaches of equalities or anti-discrimination laws where a purported exercise of academic freedom may be a factor in adjudicating whether the expression reasonably had the prohibited effect. There are well-founded arguments, however, given that in Shahvisi's analysis incivility hinges on domination, to extend the interference in academic freedom of expression to cases of bullying, defined by the Advisory, Conciliation and Arbitration Service (ACAS) in the UK as an abuse or misuse of power that undermines, humiliates, or causes emotional or physical harm. In practice, many university conduct or "dignity" policies in the UK do this and typically go even further in regulating "unacceptable" conduct, though there has been considerable challenge from different parts of the political spectrum to the rhetoric of "courteousness" (the British pronunciation of civility?) or "respect."

Intuitively, the hearing that academics get—their authority and credibility is to a large extent dependent on uptake—seems to demand that they assume some responsibility for the epistemic effects of their speech. In the eyes of the ECtHR and other European and international bodies, respect for the dignity of the person need not conflict with the critical attitude required to maintain academics' specific epistemic role as disseminators of knowledge, intellectual innovators, and watchdogs in democratic societies. If anything, "tolerance"—the alternative proposed in the University of Cambridge affair over "respect"— feels somewhat out of tune with that epistemic justification if it is taken as a desired comportment not simply toward others (in which case it is arguably condescending or demeaning) but more crucially toward *ideas*, for it is surely incumbent upon an academic to be *intolerant* of bad or ill-founded ideas.

But exactly what should be tolerated, let alone respected, in the name of academic freedom? Can academics mouth off about anything and with any degree of expertise or skill? Does it matter who might be listening? While there is some common ground on what professional standards might be, there are also significant variations and disagreements. Strasbourg has defined the scope of academic freedom as falling within an academic's "areas of research, professional expertise and competence"—somewhat wider than the notion, oft cited and questioned in the United States, of "credentialed scholarly expertise" or the controversial "field of expertise" in an early version of the UK Bill, which was intended to capture the spirit of that ECtHR judgment but was removed under cross-bench and lobby-group pressure.[12] Most objections to that narrow scope pointed out the epistemic value, for the academy and beyond, of interdisciplinary cross-fertilization and of innovation at the leading edge of disciplines, not to mention the expertise that academics acquire in pedagogy and the broader competence they may obtain through committee service and public engagement. (Having drafted a new policy on academic freedom and navigated the various compliance, assurance, and governance issues associated with it, these are now presumably new strings to my bow in addition to my core areas of research and teaching.) The Strasbourg Court, though, has shown little appetite for the AAUP position that extramural speech be protected, regardless of whether it flows from expertise, provided it does not bear upon an academic's fitness for professional service. In addition to limiting the scope by competence or expertise, Strasbourg case law shows the Court ready to impose standards of professional conduct and ethics on academics (as it does on journalists) and to recognize the capacity of professions to self-determine these standards. The fact that an academic book conformed to scholarly standards was, for example, pivotal in a majority judgment in a case of alleged negative stereotyping of Roma.[13]

In Anglophone contexts, an expressly disciplinary conception of these standards tends to prevail. Shahvisi, for example, endorses the requirement that academic research "meet particular methodological standards" required for publication and "rest on an accepted evidence-base" defensible through due regard to existing literature, and that teaching and outreach be grounded in that research. These fairly traditional limits on academic freedom leave considerable scope for disciplinary gatekeeping. They are often used as a pretext for excluding scholars of color from tenure and promotion where their work in no way falls short of those standards but challenges them or exposes the assumptions on which they rely. Aside from discrimination, such standards risk maintaining a certain conformity of disciplinary reproduction whereby the transition from one state of the field to a new one requires that those espousing the earlier views already have reasons for adopting the new proposals. Even when conceived more capaciously than a "settled body of knowledge," disciplinarity is a bridle to thinking otherwise. For Foucault, whose own practice is thoroughly de-disciplinarizing, a discipline, in addition to being delimited by a domain of objects, methods, corpuses, rules, definitions, instruments, and techniques, defines itself through the admissibility of propositions: "A proposition must fulfil some onerous and complex conditions before it can be admitted within a discipline; before it can be pronounced true or false it must be, as Monsieur Cauguilhem might say, 'within the true.'"[14] And yet he also highlights how this discursive policing is premised on the limitless possibility of novel statements whose legitimacy it is the task of disciplinarity to determine: "For a discipline to exist, there must be the possibility of formulating—and of doing so ad infinitum—new propositions."[15]

The question is whether disciplinary enforcement of standards—Postian or otherwise—is a reasonable trade-off or the most appropriate mechanism for preserving the robustness of scholarship.[16] Joan Wallach Scott has been a consistent voice defending the value of expertise yet cautioning against according excessive sanctity to disciplinarity, lest it bar "those most likely to have remade the field."[17] Appeals to disciplinarity effectively make AFOE conditional upon the field of (tenured) scholars having ears already predisposed to hear a novel argument, say, in such a way that they already have reasons to accept those claims—or that they find the argument reason enough. It is surely possible that the very fact of hearing something unforeseen, and even unforeseeable, can be what provides reasons to accept it. In other words, if one subscribes to a disciplinary analysis, it can also be the very exercise of academic freedom as a challenge to the existing state of the field that can create the conditions of its legitimation. On this analysis, disciplinarity would be somewhat *nachträglich*, or belated, its discipline somewhat syncopated with itself, even a little bit indisciplined—and not by accident.

Shahvisi, though, does not limit herself to the conventional disciplinary standards. She further argues that, in order to minimize misuse or abuse of epistemic privilege, scholarly argument needs to be sufficiently rigorous and also to anticipate, judiciously rehearse, and rebut any potential counterarguments. The apparent sovereign freedom of disciplinary innovation that I just outlined comes undone on its own retroactive legitimation—and this is the very aporia of institutionalization, of foundation, of constituted and constitutive power, of the transcendental, in short. Shahvisi's second set of stipulations instead openly embraces the prostheticity of academic freedom in requiring a mode of argumentation inherently sensitive to a responsiveness of and to the other. Otherwise put, listening is implicated in the standards for academic freedom in the form of a mutual hearing of reasons and counter-reasons—a hearing, in other words, that always already invites another hearing, and thus a kind of over-hearing of hearing with all the dangers that entails.

If hearing of this sort is implied in the concept of academic freedom, that commitment to counterargument should perhaps extend to the very disciplinary norms that decide which methods, evidence, and literature are acceptable so as to avoid the notorious gatekeeping function of peer review. The 2020 Bonn Declaration on Freedom of Scientific Research recognizes this dilemma when it states that, while informed by disciplinary standards, academic freedom also enables academics to challenge those standards as new inquiry begins to question their validity.[18] If a challenge to disciplinary standards is a legitimate exercise of academic freedom only when that challenge is deemed acceptable by the yardstick of disciplinary authorities, this would preserve an inherently conservative tendency that contradicts the oft-cited social justification for the special protections academics enjoy: namely, to expand the breadth of knowledge, information, and evidence available for deliberation in a democratic society.

But before we rush to embrace this presumption against disciplinarity, there is also a counterargument that epistemic concerns warrant careful scrutiny of innovative or experimental research according to tried-and-tested ways of doing scholarship lest it turn out to be *epistemically vicious*, for example because it is bullshit, sophistry, or dogma. Such concerns tend to motivate calls to regulate the quality of argumentation, rather than, say, the content, method, or literature cited—and yet there are plenty who would tell me that Derrida fails to meet the requisite standards of philosophical argumentation! Trans scholars have pointed out that Kathleen Stock's struggle to publish work on gender in peer-reviewed venues might be because she hasn't done the reading (a charge that couldn't be leveled against Derrida).[19] One might therefore argue that she cannot fall back on the enhanced level of protection afforded by Strasbourg to AFOE, although a high level of protection is afforded, in any event, to nonacademic expression on political or public-interest matters. One response might be that academic freedom entails choosing one's own authorities and citational practices, though at what point would clinging to discredited authorities (and who has the authority to discredit them?) or failing to engage counterarguments fatally wound the quality of one's argument to such a degree that it should forfeit that special protection? Academic freedom is, in part, meant to protect intellectual experiments, such as venturing into new areas of inquiry, but then it might appear to be an abuse of that authority prematurely to hold oneself out as an expert rather than an apprentice. This is what has provoked allegations of "hubris" in Stock's case for what looks like an unwillingness to recognize what one does not know.

A related kind of intellectual hubris, often cited in ethics codes, entails treating other scholars unfairly, such as failing to acknowledge their intellectual contribution or unduly misrepresenting their arguments. The former seems straightforward, but strong reading—or even willful or creative misreading when not designed to deceive—is an accepted, even respected, method in some fields, where it operates as an engine of critical and novel thought. The possibility of academic freedom and its risk of vice thus turns, in many ways, on the practice of reading or what I prefer to think of as *readlistening* to a text, tradition, argument, archive, data, testimony, and so on because it is suggestive of auscultating these bodies as to sound them out, for good or ill health, in ways that are differential, resisting totalization. It entails *tapping* them in the multiple senses discussed in the previous chapter of tapping Black rage. In Geoff Bennington's elucidation of Derrida's method (if it can be called such a thing), texts contain resources beyond, and that may even contradict, the readings they themselves propose. In saying one thing a text may advertise itself to be heard as saying another, while, in fact, a keen listener is able to pick out yet another thought. For deconstruction, what I'm calling readlistening always falls short when it stops at taking the speaker as saying what they intended to be understood. There must be scope for mishearing in uptake. And yet if one rushes into listening against the grain without any regard for the advertised interpretation, one also misses out on the full intellectual fruits of taking a speaker to be saying what they understand themself to be saying while at the same time taking them as saying what they fail to hear in themselves. The ethical negotiation of that gap, which is, at heart, a matter of listening, is the engine of intellectual inquiry.

One counterargument to this worry about overly adventurous readlistening might be that it is for philosophy, as a discipline, to sanction this method, and yet it is, of course, a major point of fracture in the discipline, so much so that some who exercise it have found themselves exiled to other departments or job insecurity. Derrida's model, however, challenges the very idea of an academic community predicated on consensus and the safe borders it appears to afford. Instead, in a slight twist to the Bonn Declaration, deconstruction offers up for thought the idea that disciplinarity, if it is to be disciplined enough, will always be its own undoing. This is why when, as part of university strategy, we debate the definitions of multi-, inter-, and transdisciplinary, I always like to say, only half-jokingly, that I'm a fan of indisciplinarity. Far from needing to open up discipline from outside, there is no discipline that is not always already destined to indiscipline itself to a certain degree. A discipline so rigorously disciplined that it were not open to the other beyond its borders would be too intellectually brittle to withstand the negotiation of counterargument and rebuttal—the very life of thought. A discipline without any sense of its boundaries would be too flaccid to stand up to that kind of jousting, hence my intuition that disciplinarity is necessarily always somewhat, yet never wholly, indisciplined.

As Bennington argues, it is sovereignty that is the greatest resistance to this type of reading, which he identifies, following Derrida, with democracy.[20] This is not exactly the dissensual democracy that Miguel de Beistegui, for example, defends; Rancièran dissensus is already too resolvable in its dialectic or oppositionality.[21] One need not be a deconstructionist, though, to argue for the epistemic virtues of open-mindedness. The typical offenses against academic standards—often because they offend the principle of open-minded inquiry—are not immediately recognizable as instances of sovereign will or autonomy, although I shall be arguing that they have something of that about them. To my knowledge no court or tribunal has yet to consider whether bullshit (in Harry Frankfurt's sense) qualifies as an exercise of academic freedom. In an article arguing against no-platforming in general and specifically for deemed breach of disciplinary axioms or want of disciplinary competence, Uwe Peters and Nikolaj Nottelman nonetheless take as "uncontroversial" the exclusion from academic spaces of a category of speakers in addition to those whose expression is or is highly likely to be unlawful. These include individuals "known to offer only positions/arguments devoid of meaning, and to intend to bedazzle audience members ignorant of relevant terminologies and discursive norms," such as by producing bullshit, or those "known to try to proliferate harmful/false views . . . by way of manipulation [e.g., by rhetoric] rather than coherent arguments."[22]

Without specifically explaining this assumption, in dismissing certain arguments in favor of no-platforming Peters and Nottelman insist on the epistemic merits of exposure to "authentic dissent," which they distinguish from both playing devil's advocate and manufacturing doubt—both mere imitations of dissent because they supposedly have little interest in the truth value of the claims at stake or even in their defensibility. While the authors don't make a substantive argument for the exclusion of bullshit, bedazzlement, or other manipulation—it is, ironically, of the order of the rhetorically asserted taken-as-understood!— their overall argument implies that those categories of expression are disqualified by their impact on a listener's relation to the truth. By contrast, authentic dissent is pivotal for truth tracking, their argument goes, even when it perpetuates falsehood because it offers the best version of the position—the most accurate and committed representation and, ideally, the most skillfully argued—and thus more effectively enables listeners to form robust counterarguments, strengthen defenses of the position challenged, and submit its underlying assumptions to renewed critical scrutiny. Those who wonder why three Ivy league presidents acquitted themselves so poorly in the face of leading questioning at the congressional committee might ponder these arguments about the epistemic effects of propaganda or manipulation.

The argument for hearing out authentic dissent bears comparison with Quassim Cassam's rejection of the claim that closed-mindedness can sometimes be necessary to protect knowledge. Those who are closed-minded, he notes, are "less inclined to listen" or to revise their views in light of what they hear.[23] Their undue desire for closure and intolerance of ambiguity has something in common with sovereignty, which shuts itself off from difference, within or without, and is similarly resistant to listening. Cassam's argument against closed-mindedness, however, turns on a minimal integrity of the knowing subject. Cassam argues that dogmatism is not required to protect knowledge unless one were to fear that one might be seduced by propaganda, conspiracy theory, or sophistry into giving up one's convictions or at least into losing one's right to feel confident in them.[24] The intellectual danger in such cases is not, therefore, a surfeit of open-mindedness or exposure to "bad" dissent but a lack of epistemic self-confidence. A determination to avoid, disregard, or dismiss out of hand false or misleading evidence lest it contradict what one knows might suggest that one isn't so sure that one knows after all, meaning that regardless of whether one encounters propaganda or bullshit, one's right to be confident in what one knows and hence one's knowledge are already on the ropes.

Open-mindedness, Cassam suggests, should be distinguished from an intellectual "flaccidity" that poses just as much risk to knowledge as closed-mindedness.[25] Open-mindedness isn't uncritical and doesn't open the floodgates to relativism. It is entirely compatible with an intellectual tenacity or conviction that is still amenable to reconsideration and refutation but that doesn't abandon its position at the first hint of challenge without critical testing. In a similar vein, and from an expressly antifascist position, David Palumbo-Liu proposes a "litmus test" for distinguishing the exercise of academic freedom from its abuse designed solely to create spectacle and obtain a veneer of legitimacy. The latter's rhetoric "is not subtle, nuanced, open to adjustment, correction, engagement—it is brittle, bombastic, demagogic. It speaks in absolutes and tricks one into thinking that the only way to win the argument is to be equally crude, simplistic and dogmatic."[26]

In short, such speech might be considered undeserving of enhanced AFOE protections insofar as it leaves little room for a nuanced or critical response. It puts the listener in an impossible position, giving them no option but to *take it or leave it*. This phrase occurs in some fascinating remarks on academic freedom that Derrida makes in his lecture "Otobiographies" on Nietzsche. Picking up on Nietzsche's aural metaphor, he suggests that when it comes to classical pedagogy one can neither simply put one's fingers in one's ears nor listen (*hören*) with too much *Gehorsamkeit* (obedience). Derrida quips: "As everyone knows, by the terms of academic freedom—I repeat: a-ca-dem-ic freedom—you can take it or leave it."[27] These remarks encapsulate Derrida's approach to disciplinarity. If one is not to take canonical knowledge too uncritically, one necessarily takes one's leave of it without entirely rejecting or leaving it behind. In this way the idea of negative freedom as freedom from constraint—*You can take it or leave it, up to you!*—is exposed if not as false, then at least as misguided. The "or" here produces a polarization into two alternative postures that are both rather brittle or dogmatic, each closing its ears to the possibility of a more complicated and differential force field of ideas and counterarguments. Such a relation between academic freedom and disciplinarity might be better characterized as an infinite negotiation—a negotiation with imperatives from which one cannot break absolutely if one wishes to remain intelligible but which, if followed slavishly, would lead only to silence, tautology, and tedium.

Cassam envisages a similarly tireless, though not necessarily infinite, negotiation with evidence that does not simply take it or leave it. He wonders if this asks too much, though ultimately he concludes that the responsibility to make the effort to distinguish truth from lie is a necessary one, and not only for academics. But can this be a universal expectation? As he acknowledges, work on epistemic injustice has explored how individual prejudice or institutional and structural forms of marginalization can erode credibility and self-confidence, with negative epistemic impacts. One might then wonder whether expressions of closed-mindedness that have the aim or effect of significantly undermining the intellectual convictions of minorities should be excluded from the scope of academic freedom protections on the grounds that they are harmful to the collective pursuit of knowledge.[28] Alternatively, one might query where the burden of the cognitive and affective labor of refuting sophistry, conspiracy theory, and propaganda should fall when academic labor already falls disproportionately heavily on those most likely to be silenced by closed-minded and over-confident prejudice and bigotry. Since epistemic vices can be oppressive, must one negotiate with one's oppressor? By contrast, university presidents and vice-chancellors are paid handsomely to defend the integrity of academic inquiry from corruption.

If academic freedom requires a disposition open to critique, correction, and refinement, the question remains how to combat—and to what extent to protect—academic expression that is not simply indifferent to the truth, such as bullshit, but is more actively and perniciously corrosive of it, especially when it may even avail itself of the trappings of the pursuit of truth in order to manipulate. The suggested clause in the consultation response on which I commented (with due rigor, I hope) opted for a requirement that academic freedom "be exercised in accordance with recognised professional principles of intellectual rigor, scientific inquiry, and research ethics and integrity" and—at my suggestion to guard against fraud and sophistry—does "not extend to an exercise of such freedoms which purports to satisfy the requirements of this clause but which falls far below nationally and internationally accepted standards for such requirements." On Mill's analysis, this would be an incredibly difficult offense to "bring home to conviction."[29] While identifying sophistry—the mimicry of truth—as the gravest abuse of freedom of expression, he is nonetheless skeptical that it is possible to assign moral culpability or legally to regulate such infractions. This is because he thinks that when a speaker withholds facts, misstates parts of their case, or mischaracterizes their opponent's argument, they largely do so in good faith and without in general being ignorant or incompetent.

It is sometimes held that academic freedom should expressly include a right to err, otherwise it would disincentivize risk-taking in research. Presumably this is intended to extend only to errors made in good faith, which, at least in commercial contexts, is an objective test, so it ought to exclude situations where an apparent error gives the academic in question significant advantage over the person with whom they disagree or would put that person at an unfair disadvantage, for example by unduly undermining their credibility. And yet it is unclear to me whether sophistry coincides with trickery and hence with bad faith, or whether it might also be understood as know-how, or even a certain competence, in arguing that draws upon rhetoric as a tool of the trade. This goes back to the issue, discussed in chapter 2, of whether truth-telling can be cleanly distinguished from rhetoric or whether, in fact, to imagine that it can be, as a desire for purity, certainty, and clear boundaries, is a form of dogmatism or closed-mindedness. The thought would be that to imagine there is truth without risk of falsity, methodological rigor without risk of error, or truth-telling without risk of rhetorical manipulation, is itself a *ruse of (sovereign) reason* (double genitive—as both a ruse that tricks reason and a certain trickery that is not contingent but internal to reason). This isn't an invitation to abandon discerning judgment (which is what distinguishes academic from ordinary freedom of expression), rather to underscore that, in the absence of a universal prophylactic, the responsibility to discern on each occasion, conditioned and conditional as every judgment necessarily is, is even greater.

Good faith is no more fitting a test. While it may be appropriate for contracts or even the open marketplace of ideas, the epistemic justifications for the specific status of academic freedom militate against this proposal. This is because falsity, error, ignorance, lack of rigor or disciplinary competence, or even lack of integrity (where it causes no harm to others) are not inherent obstacles to *learning*—which is the supposed epistemic goal of academic inquiry and discussion—and may even be formative hurdles provided they are amenable to testing and correction. A problem arises with sophistry, dogmatism, propaganda, and so on insofar as they seek to disarm this critical faculty and to render error, falsity, laxity, and even fraud less detectable. To this extent, the litmus test ought to concern less the content or manner of speaking than the kind of listening it is capable of eliciting. While ears take in what they hear and thereby learn by taking instruction, as the phrase has it, they can also unlearn (on the basis of) what they hear.

To put it differently, the kinds of expression that arguably ought to lie outside academic freedom are those that foreclose *free listening*. Sophistry and propaganda share with dogmatism a preconceived outcome. They seek to deny room for the negotiation of which Derrida speaks and instead persuade to their advantage and to win over, whatever the cost to learning and knowledge. In short, they offend against the open-mindedness of free inquiry by seeking to determine in advance what is acceptable. It seems fairly obvious that ideas that do not come to have the status of knowledge or discoveries for a particular discipline or that come to be deemed incomplete or erroneous can still play an important role in shaping what comes to be accepted knowledge in that discipline. It cannot therefore be the case that academic freedom protects only what is already accepted or even would, on Foucault's definition of discipline, already be accepted. In part this is because the rejection of views and the discovery of error and ignorance is part and parcel of the process of disciplinary formation and reproduction such that disciplines necessarily include their margins and exclusions. Further, it is quite possible that the reasons to accept a particular claim might become available only with the making of that claim.

Moreover, making the vindication of new ideas dependent on existing or preauthorized ones condemns disciplinarity to a regression toward a transcendental condition on which that series cannot retroact and hence is beyond rational vindication: that is, an event of sovereign self-founding. One school of thought predominant in nineteenth-century aesthetics, for example, has it that innovation beyond convention, creativity outside of norms, is the possession of a sovereign genius, freedom from external constraint or pressure. And yet this ignores the fact that what appears as something singular and unprecedented is a *response* both to prevailing conditions and to something unpredictable that surprises even the apparent "author" of invention—a response to what one has, in advance, no good reason to accept. In short, the need for academic freedom to protect the unforeseeable and the as-yet-unacceptable means that its disciplinary definition is already ruined in advance—or we have to accept that there is no disciplinarity worthy of the name that is not always already a bit indisciplined.

Even if epistemic deficiencies are irreducible, is there, nonetheless, reason to exclude what de Beistegui categorizes as the *noetically* vicious—that is, a more general intellectual incompetence not restricted to disciplinary knowledge? Focusing on the examples of stupidity, superstition, and spite, he argues that such vices are pre-epistemic and are concerned not with the distinction between truth and error but, drawing on the later Foucault, with the moment of problematization that precedes yet tends to be obscured by knowledge. Moreover, these are not accidental but internal to reason, its blind spots or deaf points. Transcendentally vicious, stupidity in de Beistegui's terms is not ignorance or deficiency of understanding or judgment but a power internal to intelligence that undoes itself by asking useless or badly posed problems or questions or by otherwise suppressing them.[30] Reflecting the significance of indetermination or openness, he specifies that a well-constructed problem necessarily exceeds its (hypothetical) solution.

Who, though, gets to decide what is stupidity? The attribution of *bêtise*, to accuse someone of being *bête*—the French word that is translated as "stupid" but also has the sense of "animal" or "beastly," though it is therefore only humans and not beasts that can be *bête*—ought to behoove a certain modesty, as Gilles Deleuze suggests.[31] Deleuze's insinuation that philosophy is not immune to stupidity is at the heart of de Beistegui's argument; yet he doesn't pursue its full ramifications. If Deleuze separates *bêtise* from error, Derrida (tracking this beast of *bêtise* in Deleuze) makes a point about the more Kantian conception of stupidity as want of judgment, or an aptitude to make poor judgments "through precipitation of the will disproportionate to the understanding . . . to the point of vertigo, of a *bêtise* that . . . lets itself be touched and moved by a certain infinity of freedom."[32] Sovereignty's imperviousness to difference would, on this reading, be the source of such stupidity. But Derrida also notes that *bêtise* is not only a character trait but, without simply being an error, something I can do by accident, surprising myself—a whoopsie—or something unaccountable for which no one is to blame. It also has the sense of being a bit slow on the uptake (Derrida uses the French slang *comprenure*). As such, it can sit on the side of listening, even if it is betrayed in speaking.

If *bêtise* is neither a univocal concept nor stable in its position-ality, this is also because the accuser and the accused cannot be so cleanly separated. Philosophy ought to be modest because when it spies stupidity, it should also look in the mirror. *Bêtise* is contagious. That doesn't, though, make it hapless error or illusion. It is, rather, a ruse or stratagem of mastery, even if it is an illusion of pulling and pulled strings in which the listener participates. Derrida's point is that it is the sovereign, whom we tend to distinguish from the beast, who is most *bête* in that fiction, precisely because he thinks that he alone is immune and hence doesn't get the originary implication of the other— for which listening is but one name. One might then say that sovereign freedom is a bit slow on the uptake, slow to get that there is even something like uptake, at least beyond the execu-tion of the performative.

Common to many of the arguments considered in this chapter is an appeal to freedom as (somewhat qualified) openness, open-mindedness, or open-endedness. The examples of stupidity de Beistegui gives (prejudice, bigotry, diktat, *doxa*, unquestioned authority) all suffer from premature closure. If academic freedom has a social justification, then this openness serves to safeguard democracy, which in de Beistegui's analysis is characterized less by consensus, which can be cultivated via no end of vices (noetic, epistemic, and moral), than by dissensus, which is generous and expansive, and keeps problems alive. Stupidity, by contrast, is a kind of dogmatism that bows to the Gramscian common sense of naturalized hegemonic ideology. This means that if listen-ing is the condition of (im)possibility of expression, it must be thought beyond the horizon of uptake, beyond recognizing someone as saying something, into the far more undecidable realm of the perlocutionary discussed briefly in chapter 1. In distinguishing perlocution from illocution, Daniele Lorenzini makes a conceptual distinction between recognition, which entails the other, and the "grammar of acknowledgement," which involves mutuality and hence opens onto the "we." The minimal recognition that secures uptake is necessary but insufficient for perlocutionary effects, which are "structurally open to renegotiation."

From the perspective of this book, what Lorenzini describes are two kinds of listening, one that is apparently sovereign in that it calculates its boundaries in advance and, hence, confines itself to a predetermined circuit, the other differential in that it takes the form of a conversation with open-ended and unforeseeable potential effects. Uncritical assertation is capable of recognition (one can take someone as asserting dogmatically), but it tends to constrain the sphere of perlocutionary effects to little more than take-it-or-leave-it. The issue, though, *pace* Lorenzini, is not that bare assertion fails to construct a "we," but what kind of "we." The lesson of Trumpism should warn us that mimetic expression does so all too easily. Mimetic contagion constructs a homogeneous "we" as false totality, a ruse of sovereignty (national, racial, and so on). Such expression leaves no room for listening to anything more than realizing or thwarting a promise whose potential resolution is already determined—hence the mythological-destinal features of nationalisms. The listener isn't free to re-pose the problem anew or differently. Listening, as such, is denied the freedom to problematize or to renegotiate the terms of the problem; there is just loss or (impossible) restitution, whence the manic-melancholic affect of dogmatic expression.

The urge to separate pursuit of the truth from politics and its trappings, not least rhetoric, shares with dogmatism a will to purify. But a key claim of this book is that it's necessary to liberate freedom from purification, which also means that freedom will always be an improvised, open-ended, and renegotiated liberation, never settled once and for all. To see (academic) freedom as always irreducibly conditional and conditioned is also to return it to the sphere of labor struggles, because it is the nature of the employment relationship, from precarity to the relative financial security of tenure, that determines the degree of liberty to express one's views without fear of detriment or reprisal. According to one classical formulation that prioritizes freedom from external interest, academic freedom justifies its special status on the basis of its freedom from all social, demo-cratic, or material conditions rather than its socio-democratic utility. This ruse of freedom as the disinterested pursuit of truth feigns to rise, as Julia Schleck has argued in an earlier volume in this Provocations series, above the fray of material interests in the world and the imbalance of power between capital and labor, whereas in reality academia has always been in the business of producing "dirty knowledge."[33] Behind intellectual or aesthetic disinterestedness is a secret or repressed interest.

This intuition leads her to suspect the normative and univer-sal impulses of a rights-based definition of academic freedom. But one reason, *pace* Schleck, to preserve academic freedom as a species of human right rather than as an employment rela-tion—or, more precisely, as a right that inheres both within and without employment contracts—is that it puts the question of standing on the agenda. It thereby encapsulates situations in which there is a political struggle to acquire and retain mem-bership in the academic communities said to reproduce the conditions for academic freedom. Academic freedom is not a transhistorical idea, but Schleck's strongly periodizing historiog-raphy, with its multiple gestures of inauguration (neoliberalism brings about a rupture, we need a "new" freedom, and so on), discovers apparent novelties in marketization and the de facto abolition of tenure that have always been symptomatic of liberty in its modern and pre-modern guises. Derrida might say that this kind of claim has a whiff of sovereignty about it. There is, of course, also an argument to be made that listening to and for academic freedom would need to be liberated from a human-rights framework such that the freedom is not only the property of a recognized liberal subject with standing from a juridical point of view. This substratum of belonging that conditions academic freedom means that it is ripe, as history has shown, for marginalization and exclusion. And yet one can no more oppose sovereignty hastily and frontally than one can purify academic reason of dishonesty or fiction. The abolitionism advocated in this book is, rather, a slow and differentiated task that shatters sovereign freedom on the rocks of other minor freedoms and sovereignties. Conceiving of academic freedom as an infinite praxis of negotiation, challenge, openness, and risk-taking takes a step toward freeing the hearing that academics get from the false totalities of imagined communities and authoritarian sovereignties.

6

Unheard

Silence, Justice, Repair

One of the most significant exercises of academic freedom in recent decades has entailed pushing at the boundaries of sanctioned disciplinary methodologies in a bid to repair their complicity with forms of oppression and exclusion. Notwithstanding the visibility of a small number of queer, Black, Brown, and otherwise marginalized academics, such uses of academic freedom, no doubt insofar as they expose the complicity of self-appointed gatekeepers in the field, continue to put scholars at risk of being denied tenure or entry to the profession in the first place. Such complicities with structural oppression have often, though not exclusively, manifested themselves as lacunae that remain imperceptible from within the horizon of disciplinarity. These zones of inaudibility mark the double *différend* of a disciplinarity insufficiently reflexive to hear its own silencing mechanisms. It is for this reason that simply multiplying perspectives—the "viewpoint diversity" championed by the right or even the marketplace of ideas to which many liberals remain attached—is no remedy, for it fails to rebalance the structural inaudibility of certain voices within that field. It relies upon the fiction of a vocal equality that does not exist and is more than accidentally impaired. Moreover, it remains committed, as a matter of principle, to continuing to platform voices that perpetuate forms of oppression and promulgating expression that has the effect of silencing or undermining the audibility of other forms of expression.

Insofar as academic freedom, understood as a form of post-Kantian criticality, is discerning as to the epistemic or noetic value of expression, though not to its content or the subject position of the speaker, it has a corrective, or one might even say reparative, potential. It is, in theory, capable of tearing down its own foundations and presuppositions to make room to rebuild new institutions of knowledge and inquiry. And yet, as I have explored elsewhere, the limits of the criticist account of academic freedom from a deconstructionist perspective are that it is unable to challenge the conditions of its own foundation.[1] By contrast, the position I'm staking out in this book follows Derrida in insisting on "the possibility of suspending in an argued, deliberated, rational fashion, all conditions, hypotheses, conventions, and presuppositions, and of criticizing unconditionally all conditionalities, including those that still found the critical idea."[2] The silence of critique, then, is the silence of critique. That is, the matter on which it remains silent, has nothing to say, is its own silence and hence complicities with structural silencing. Only the experimental borrowing or invention of other forms of inquiry outside of disciplinarity and outside even the practice of critique altogether can offer something like responsibility or justice.

The silences of the archive are not accidents of history. The documents lost, the memories erased, the voices suppressed, the forms of narration eclipsed, the violence forgotten—all are structural features of history's condition of possibility as a discipline that curates its story according to prevailing distributions of audibility. It is because there have historically been no (and to this day still too few) ears for voices of the enslaved that their stories do not speak to us through scholarly history today. They are not silent because they have nothing to say. They are inaudible because white ears have found nothing to hear in anything that exceeds a reassuring resonance and might percuss them with calls for response-ability. Saidiya Hartman, an African American scholar known for her creative practices of reconstructing the "cultivated silences" of the archive, observes that redressing this inaudibility requires "turning to forms of knowledge and practice not generally considered legitimate objects of historical inquiry or appropriate or adequate sources for history making."[3] Hartman variously describes what she does as "raiding," "misshaping," "deforming," spinning new narratives out of the scraps that remain and by selectively quoting and amplifying,[4] and, in the text that would inscribe her work within the canon of historiographic practice, as "critical fabulation."[5]

The focus on stories urges a drift toward aurality that isn't necessarily privileged in her work. First, drawing upon an ocular metaphor as she attends to the critical or dismantling part of her project, Hartman says that she aims to "make *visible*" how history and its fictions have participated in "the production of disposable lives." Then, in a second move, aiming to describe what Fred Moten has called the "resistance of the object," Hartman turns to the ear, figuring the imagination as an aural capacity "to listen for the mutters and oaths and cries of the commodity [and] to engulf authorized speech in the clash of voices."[6] Critical fabulation is perhaps something of a misnomer for Hartman's practice since her art of the *fabula*, which derives from *fari*, meaning to speak, both attests to and is predicated on a certain refraining from speaking or telling the story to make way for aural attunement, to "listen for the unsaid," "listen for the groans and cries, the undecipherable songs, the crackle of fire in the cane fields, the laments for the dead, and the shouts of victory, and then [NWS: and only then] assign words to all of it."[7] If listening comes first, logically if not temporally, then it makes sense that Hartman's practice is not about "giving voice." Instead, it looks rather like the kind of response-ability that I have been arguing offers a more genuine emancipation than free speech.

Hartman understands her practices to be deeply entangled with what she calls the "incomplete project of freedom" but not because they liberate the voices they exhume as if from burial in an unmarked tomb. Hartman sees, with burning perspicacity, the intimate affiliation of liberty and enslavement insofar as the liberal construction of freedom is predicated upon property, its prized autonomy on self-possession. If redressing the lacunae of the archive is at once, for Hartman, to write a history of the present, this is not because, from some enlightened vantage point of recognition and remorse, historians today might free the voices of the past from captivity. Rather, it is the "intimacy" of experiences today with the lives of the dead, disturbing our present now, that promises an as-yet unattained horizon of liberation. The "free state" conjured up by Hartman's practice as a historian does not temporally precede enslavement but exists as the "anticipated future" of this writing. She is quick to note that these counter-histories cannot break absolutely with the narratives of domination that have censored them. The effort of reconstruction exists in struggle within and against—*tout contre*, one might say in a Derridean spirit—the silences of the archive. They might even be heard as (the power of) silence always already resisting itself.

Hartman's analysis of the intimate relation between the bondage of slavery and the freedom of the sovereign subject also illustrates why the practices of listening and narrating she advocates are not about restoring an originary state of freedom.

In this, the Black radical tradition and its legacies diverge sharply, as we shall see by comparison with normative accounts of testimonial justice in Anglophone moral philosophy, which cling to idealizations of the state of human nature in what, I shall suggest, ultimately amount to denials of structural silencing and overestimations of the corrective capacity of forms of listening that remain within the horizon of metaphysical rationality. While Hartman, in passing, wonders whether these stories are a form of reparations ("perhaps the only kind we will ever receive"), this analogy with repair, compensation, or making whole reaches its limits. She reaches instead for the notion of "redress," necessarily incomplete, the speech recovered in some sense always impossible. And to erase such impossibility would be to inflict a redoubled harm, denying the unfreedom that persists. Hartman's stories, then, cannot heal history. The repetition and recomposition of narrative fragments bear witness to a breach whose repair is infinitely deferred. The redress enacted in critical fabulation nonetheless seeks to transfigure the broken and disciplined body, even as it remembers this loss and testifies to the longing for reparation. The labor of critical fabulation is borne out of responsibility and from listening to, responding to, the gaps and the scraps in the archive. As such it has the character of what I am calling response-ability.

By this, I do not intend to elide Hartman with Derrida, to suggest that Black radical and deconstructive thought are supplements or fulfilments of one another, or could be reduced to a common theoretical horizon. Nor do I claim on the latter's behalf a long investment in the deconstruction of race and the colonial foundations of European thought, albeit motivated by his own Algerian childhood, or to make his cautious interest in abolition (of apartheid, of the death penalty) speak for abolitionism in general. Yet there is a certain affinity between deconstruction and the Black critical political imagination, though neither is a homogeneous corpus. Drawn to ellipses, both are dissenting, fugitive forms of thought that refuse to be contained and that strike at the very conditions of thinking and its foundational institutions. Both, for different reasons and from different perspectives, unravel Western rationality and find refuge in its noisy margins. For Moten, the appeal of deconstruction also lies in the fact that Derrida "wanted philosophy to *sound* like something" and, to that extent, his "blurs" with other vernaculars, while also freeing aurality from under the thumb of the *logos*.[8] At the same time as they put pressure on transcendentals, both are preoccupied by those foundational institutions and political concepts that must simultaneously come undone—democracy, liberalism, humanism. There is a rapprochement between strands of deconstructive and Black thought that dodge those logics of oppositionality that continue to haunt other forms of post-structuralist and postcolonial thought. It might seem as if one stresses *de*-construction and the other *re*-construction, with W. E. B. Du Bois's interest in creating new social institutions, for example, having more in common with Nancy's bids to recuperate the concepts of the liberal-humanist tradition. I would argue, though, that it would be a mistake to assume that Derrida is concerned only with dismantling. It is perhaps, rather, that the generative moment for him—in thinking, for instance, of the democracy to come—is characterized less as rebuilding since it must necessarily be open to chance beyond calculation and cannot be cleanly separated from the shattering force of dissemination. While Du Bois, and Angela Davis after him, admittedly do not prescribe the form that this new democracy should take, Davis evokes radical experimentation.[9] More poetic strains of Black studies, including Black feminisms, find their waywardness in coordinates uncharted by or that swerve away from Eurocentric philosophical categories.

If there is some sense of recuperation, of recovery, in the multiple wakes of the Black radical tradition, it lies less in restoring than in transforming, displacing the silences. Although Hartman might not express it in this way, from the perspective set out in this book, the form of listening required has a certain faith that the silences are not absences, erasures, or empty voids. The theory of silence at stake therefore does not categorize it straightforwardly as nothingness or pure negativity, even if this is how the history of European metaphysics is structured— around a lack, a void, a vanishing ground whose disappearance is to be forgotten. Redress entails an act of faith that silence is not simply absence, negation, repression, nor the pure other or the birthplace of language. Once one instead realizes that silence has something to say—that it perhaps, if anything, has too many things to say—its creative possibilities and its capacities for driving radical social and political change begin to surface.

Derrida addresses the topic of silence and what might, after Catherine Malabou, be called its "plasticity" in both a very early seminar from 1959–60 taught at Lycée le Mans, whose dense philosophical and literary references must have baffled his post-Bac "*hypokhâgne*" class, and also in a long-form interview conducted with Alexander García Düttmann thirty years later.[10] Both manuscripts remain unpublished but can be consulted at the Institut Mémoires de l'édition contemporaine, which is housed in the restored Abbaye d'Ardenne in Caen, Normandy, where twenty Canadian soldiers were executed by the Twelfth ss Panzer Division Hitlerjugend—a fact that calls to be uttered given the interview's preoccupation with philosophical silences on the atrocities of Nazism. On both occasions, Derrida ponders how silence is signifying, suggesting that one might even speak of a language of silences and not only of silence as the vanishing condition of possibility of language. Insofar as silence may signify many things, and even the same silence may, in different contexts or to different audiences, signify different things, there is not one silence or "the" silence but many, and there is no unity to this multiplicity, no single concept that would encompass them all adequately. I can refrain from speaking out of fear or out of discretion or politeness, for example. Silence can indicate approval or contempt. I might not know how to respond or might be refusing to do so. I might be silent out of amazement or despair, acquiescence or confusion. A silence may reflect that someone is uncomfortable in a situation or it may be the sign of the most contented and intimate communion among lovers. Keeping silence may be cowardice or an act of great courage. And it goes on, the silences multiplying.

Historian Theo Jung gives a fascinating account, for example, of the ways in which the significance of silences changed in response to political events during the course of the French Revolution.[11] Once taken in political contexts to be a sign of tacit approval (*qui tacet consentire videtur*, as the saying coined by Pope Boniface in the thirteenth century goes), silence acquired a new significance, as reflected in a standing expression that rose in popularity at the time: *le silence du peuple est la leçon des rois*. Although both the phrase and the various historical silences in front of the monarch received hotly contested interpretations, the idea was that silence, besides or instead of indicating affirmation or assent, could be instructive precisely for what it did not say, even reversing into a sign of discontent and refusal. Jung cites a source observing that a "gloomy silence" meeting the king's procession was understood as "more terrible than fits of fury," indicating a breakdown in the rapport between citizens and the state as embodied in the monarch.[12] Besides functioning as a barometer of public approval or leaders' popularity, silence is frequently understood figuratively, to this day, as an absence of political representation, the absence of noisy protest a sign of despair that the popular will would go unheard. Such silences might be the calm before the revolutionary storm and, therefore, not as reassuring as the old adage would lead a leader to believe. In his adaptations to the French translations of Bentham's *The Book of Fallacies*, the Genevan state councilor Étienne Dumont wrote of ominous silences in repressive contexts: "There, the silence of the suffering often proves nothing but the excess of oppression. Complaints would not just be pointless; they would be seditious. Only despair dares to let itself be heard. In Constantinople too, the weakest murmur heralds the storm, and the revolt follows shortly. Woe to the absolute sovereign who lends his ear to this sophism. He should be ever aware of this maxim which is its antidote. *The people's silence is the lesson of kings.*"[13]

Aside from its polysemia, silence is, moreover, pronounced or expressed in many ways. It need not even be without sound or language. There is a kind of silence, Derrida is keen to point out, that exists when someone speaks too much, in idle chatter, for example, or when they are deliberately loquacious despite having, or precisely because they have, nothing to say. One can easily think of the case of the evasive politician whose words are designed to distract from, even cover up, something unsaid or unspeakable. While the early seminar focuses primarily on definitional questions and the relation between silence and language, the later interview explicitly links silence to the questions of responsibility and justice that preoccupied Derrida during the period and were the subject of the seminars that he taught around this time. The conversation frequently turns to what responsibilities the philosopher has—as a teacher, a member of the academic community, and a public intellectual—both for what they say and what they do not say. The question of an academic or public intellectual's responsibility for speech and silences—above all their own, but potentially also their response to the speech or silences of others—prompts thinking about the exercise of academic freedom specifically, even if this is not explicitly the topic of Derrida's conversation with Düttmann. It also prompts thinking about how philosophers might attend to the violence of silence and to demands for redress.

When should a philosopher shut (the fuck) up? Düttmann presses with this question, and Derrida struggles to provide a general rule, for knowing what is too much to say and what is too little, whether to say anything at all or keep silent, is a complex and difficult calculus. It is also not a question of quantity, for it is possible to allow a "sinister silence" to set in even while writing lots of public-facing articles and signing lots of petitions. At the same time, judiciously saying little while making thought-provoking links between what a scholar says and what they have written, or between their speech and their silences, might precisely be the way to open up an entire space for debate that goes in unexpected directions. In a similar vein, Derrida cautions against rushing to judge someone's silence; a verdict may be violent if it fails to take into account that keeping silent may be preferable, from some perspectives, to saying something trivial or platitudinous, which might itself be deemed to be a kind of silence. Relatedly, citational practices entail negotiating not only a politics of silencing or amplifying those voices that tend to be marginalized but, moreover, an economy of silences. To what extent should the value of another's words be weighed when not speaking in my own might be construed as silence of a kind, hiding behind citation and failing to stand by my claims, while, conversely, speaking from my own position or paraphrasing could just as easily be taking the words out of their mouth or speaking for the other?

Due consideration to the difficulties of navigating such everyday decisions in scholarly life, such as the justified critical attention that citational practices are now beginning to receive, reveals that listening and responsiveness are inextricably entangled in (self-)silencing and, hence, in the possibility of speaking freely. There is also the other inside me: whether I am capable of listening and responding to myself, and whether my silences, no less than my speech, are adequate to my thought, which could be my internal "silent" thinking or my thinking aloud to colleagues, to students, in books, in the media, and so on. Given the increased expectations of authority that come with the exercise of academic freedom, even in the extramural domain, there may be good ethical arguments for keeping silent for fear of overinflating the credibility of what might be said and lest the audience overestimate the expertise underpinning it. In this way, I might be responsive to the response of my audience. My responsibility in speaking or keeping silent would then already be a responsibility to the possibility of listening and of my speech or my silence being heard in this way or that.

Silences may be created in part by what the audience is able to hear or in fact does hear. As the interview turns to the theme of ellipsis, which evidently intrigues Düttmann, there is a fascinating discussion of the different kinds of silence created either by spelling things out in too much detail or by condensing a complex thought too quickly. Düttmann invites Derrida to reflect on whether there is not a certain effect of silencing involved when he suddenly accelerates from a slower, more demonstrative, pedagogical form of explication to a precipitation of philosophical thought condensed into a pithy formula or aphorism. Most academics and the audiences that endure their ruminations (whether students, colleagues, policymakers, or members of the general public) would agree that there can seem to be something left unsaid when a scholar moves too swiftly, as if taking something as already understood or deliberately requiring the hearer to fill in the gap. Derrida's observation that there is something missing in measured pedagogical explanation is perhaps less intuitive. Pressed to explain his reasoning, he argues that this kind of speech, while apparently more transparent to the listener, can be less "eloquent" than condensed formulation since it often says a lot of things that are already known or understood. I take from this that a silencing effect derives from the attentional quality of the listening that such speech may elicit in listeners for whom the material is quite familiar. Slow pedagogical explication, shorn of the singular idiom that is not exhausted or reducible to logical meaning, risks being forgettable and thus lapsing into the of silence of the mundane for the listener.

If the aphorism, by contrast, "says more" and lingers in the memory, it is arguably because it demands more by way of listening. It calls for a more intense form of listening, at once more critically reflective and imaginative, more responsive perhaps than reactive, questioning more than absorbing. It also leaves the meaning of what is said less certain (that is the character of its silence) and as such lends itself to promoting further and open-ended inquiry, unlike more didactic forms of speech whose silencing effects tend instead to consist in how they close down epistemic and noetic horizons. Derrida imagines a dialogue in which the ellipsis invites the listener to answer but not necessarily immediately, allowing them to "call back," thereby leaving a "resonant trace" where the other "can take the time to respond, or respond alongside, too; to move the thing." And in not responding right away, I am to call to memory what was said (or not said) and allow it time "to reason within me . . . to resonate so that my response is not immediately an echo of what has just been said." This is why poetry and tweeting are genres no less amenable to the exercise of freeing academic inquiry than a treatise, and why it is important that Black radical practices of reconstruction involve storytelling and other forms of creative fabrication.

These questions of rhetorical strategy assume a heightened

significance when they come into contact with the injustices of domination and oppression, and with demands for speech and silence to offer recognition, redress, even reparation. I am tempted to link these aphoristic philosophical condensations (often the source of much frustration to critics of the continental tradition) to the scraps, fragments, and contradictions that characterize the extant testimonies of enslaved and detained peoples. The task here, from the perspective of that future free state to which Hartmann refers, is to liberate such scraps from the spaces of enclosure (literal and figurative) to which they have been consigned. Far from being a sign of their containment or interment, the fragmented and inconsistently overlapping nature of Hartman's sources and the narratives she weaves point to the possibility of opening up to other spaces for thinking otherwise, inside and outside of the academy.

Derrida has occasion to reflect tangentially on these issues when, at the start of the second of the five cassette tapes, they begin by talking about how their last conversation, an hour and a half spent discussing silence, had itself been silenced. It had failed to record and the B-side—literally and perhaps also figuratively in the sense that, in not being recorded, it acquired the aura of B-side material (leftover, underrated, yet for that reason more rare, authentic, and cherished)—remained blank, a lacuna in the archive, requiring my own imagination to reconstruct. This fortuitous lapse prompts Derrida, while hesitant to ascribe it too much significance, to digress a little to ponder the reasons for silences in the record. It may be due to failure of the technology or degradation of the material support but, even without this, there is "the possibility for speech not to be heard," he muses. The historical record, even when perfectly recorded, may not be read, understood, received, or responded to, giving rise to "effects of silence, as if the speech had not taken place." The crucial aspect here is the risk that listening inherently brings to all speech and by which it curtails its liberty in the sense of its sovereign autonomy. Derrida goes on to make the point about the unpredictability of uptake discussed in chapter 1: that, unless the response is already anticipated in advance within the speech itself, the recording is, in some sense, kept in silence. Or rather, he suggests tantalizingly, the recording itself does not take place once and for all but anticipates, even depends upon, repeated listenings in its future. The record *just is* those listenings that attempt to hear, to understand, to respond. "Let's suppose," he jests, "that our little machines had worked and had kept everything we said, and that we didn't listen to them again, or we didn't respond, or they were of no interest. They would have been as silent as what we are trying to wake up now!"

Derrida's repeated recourse to the metaphor of awakening to describe listening's relation to silences finds fuller expression in Christina Sharpe's notion of "wake work" as a form of imagining that takes place in the wake of slavery and its erasures. Sharpe conceives of "wake" in the multiple senses of keeping vigil with the dead, an awakening of consciousness to what has gone unheard, and a line of flight in the rippling, reverberant path of the ship. At the end of this chapter, I shall explore further what this resonant, fugitive, vigilant listening to the archive might look like. For now, though, I want to mark the belatedness or *Nachträglichkeit* of the historical record, which exists only in its wake, in the ears of survivors. For Derrida and Düttmann, pondering Heidegger's unforgivable silence on the Holocaust, the question of the survivor's power to speak and to keep silent looms large. The indictment of Heidegger by Derrida's friend Philippe Lacoue-Labarthe, among many others, rests in part on Heidegger's own understanding of remaining silent, which becomes possible only when one has something to say but does not. Without this possibility of speech, there is only the muteness of inanimate objects, he proposes. Not to speak out as a witness suggests either an inadequacy of what is said compared with what is thought, a certain unsayability seemingly born in this instance of complicity or simply cowardice, or else the unthinkability of the atrocity, which, in a sense, might then vacate the thought of Heidegger, which ought to have had something to contribute beyond trite condemnation that would close off rather than open up thought. The survivor, by contrast, faces another dilemma: when I have the power to speak out (by virtue of being the one to survive), it is not necessarily just that I have such power (there is no apparent justice in *my* survival beyond or without that of others), even if I exercise that power to say something that is just. Moreover, this limit case attests to the minimal impossibility of testimony: that I cannot attest fully to what I have survived and the one who could has not survived to testify. In this limited sense, when I testify to what I have survived, I say the unsayable and, as such, I speak to say nothing, which is a kind of silence.

The disciplines of history and philosophy both partake of this impossible testimony of survivorship. Derrida even goes so far as to suggest that the entire history of philosophy, bound up as it is with listening to the silences in what is said—both what is not said and what cannot be—is the history of bringing the unsayable, even the unthinkable, to speech, and to that extent remains a kind of silence, of speaking to say nothing. The methodologies of silencing are thus critical to questions of disciplinarity and the testing of its boundaries. Notwithstanding his identity as a French Algerian Jew, Derrida is often caricatured as a philosopher obsessed by language to the point of having nothing, or too little too late, to say about injustice, domination, or oppression. In this interview, however, he addresses head on this accusation by suggesting, somewhat too sketchily but not without reason, that deconstruction is the exposing of philosophy as a kind of speaking to say nothing and thereby not simply saying nothing of the truth but concealing it or distracting from crimes such as slavery and forms of exploitation. The history of philosophy serves power in speaking to say nothing. More specifically, the charge that deconstruction levels at metaphysics and logocentrism is that all speculative idealism, insofar as it interprets and idealizes the world, silences capitalist, patriarchal, colonial, and other political violence. On a certain strong or perhaps trivializing reading, "deconstruction could consist of saying that . . . logocentric forms of hierarchization were a burning, eloquent way to remain silent on everything that this hierarchy submits to." It is here that it makes common purpose with Black radical and abolitionist imaginaries.

No doubt controversially, I want to argue that one of the most significant strains of philosophical thinking to have garnered much liberal-progressive attention in recent years suffers precisely from saying something, often quite eloquently, precisely so as to remain silent. The notions of epistemic and testimonial justice theorized by Miranda Fricker and developed by other moral philosophers flirt with this danger because of their attachment to idealization. Perhaps what is most surprising, at least from the vantage point of the argument developed in this book, is that it does so while grounding its account of epistemic virtue in a theory of listening. For this reason, it is necessary to distinguish this research from the kinds of wayward listening that I believe might abolish the silencing of oppression. My argument will, in some ways, move parallel to or crisscross Kristie Dotson's critique, which highlights, as she delicately puts it, "challenges that arise when attempting to avoid epistemic oppression, even while drawing attention to epistemic forms of oppression."[14] I will argue that Fricker's theory of epistemic injustice comes up short in failing to imagine another kind of listening besides that conceived by metaphysical humanism and logocentrism.

In her highly influential 2007 book, Fricker is concerned with two kinds of epistemic injustice, which she characterizes as testimonial and hermeneutic. Both are said to "derive from some ethical poison in the judgement of the hearer."[15] This tends, as I shall seek to show, to overlook the pharmacological intermingling of poison and remedy. The result is to reduce listening to a form of restoration and purification. The poison in the case of testimonial injustice is unacknowledged and yet morally culpable identity-based prejudice that produces a credibility deficit. The listener unduly attributes to a speaker less credibility than they otherwise would, solely on account of their identity (such as their gender or class background), and thereby wrongly undermines the speaker in their capacity as an epistemic subject or knower. Fricker's second type of epistemic injustice is more structural in character. While in testimonial injustice the ear of Fricker's vicious listener is formed under the pressure of socialization to internalize prejudices and stereotypes forged in the collective imaginary, this social formation is mediated, at least minimally, by the cognitive and affective capacities of the individual subject. In the second type, the injustice consists in rendering experiences of marginalization imperceptible on account of a lack of collective hermeneutic resources, or at least hegemonic ones. In both instances, the relative freedom of expression is determined by the conditions under which it is heard and that enable it to be more or less audible.

Whereas we might be familiar with the metaphor of (in)visibility to describe experiences of marginalization, Fricker's choice to figure epistemic injustice as an aural deficiency whose remedy lies in more virtuous modalities of hearing is an interesting one. This decision reflects the power that listening holds to determine the freedom or unfreedom of speech. Even if free speech is not her main area of concern, her analysis makes clear that it is listening that must be liberated from prejudice for there to be freedom of expression. Not unlike my distinction, in chapter 5, between open-mindedness and intellectual flaccidity, the "virtuous hearer" must be open without being credulous of testimony that is in fact false. While this is not the focus of Fricker's account, testimonial injustice undermines and erodes confidence in the epistemic system as a whole by "creating blockages in the circulation of critical ideas" or, more broadly, failing to regulate the flow of ideas in ways that are just, egalitarian, and democratic. She argues: "The fact that prejudice can prevent speakers from successfully putting knowledge into the public domain reveals testimonial injustice as a serious form of unfreedom in our collective speech situation—and on a Kantian conception, the freedom of our speech situation is fundamental to the authority of the polity, even to the authority of reason itself."[16]

The political dimension of Fricker's theory hinges on the unequal distribution of perceived authority and hence on the hearer's power to authorize or countersign what is said, and thereby to liberate expression from suspicion, distrust, and censorship. Without this differentiation, the capacity to have faith in any expression of the other, and the entire communicative apparatus that rests upon that trust, is severely imperiled. As such, the discerning judgment of the listener is not a limiting factor on speech's freedom (to say anything, and so on) but permissive: a necessary, if insufficient, condition for the confidence that lubricates its free circulation. Correctly regulating the valves of trustworthy or untrustworthy testimony is essential to keep the plumbing of democracy in good working order. It operates in the same way as an economy of credit without which the circulation of commodities would wind to a halt. (The links to religious belief and faith in the confessional, of which the ear is the primary channel, are not trivial.)

Fricker inherits this emphasis on aurality from the point at which Bernard Williams's and Edward Craig's epistemological accounts of the state of nature diverge. Whereas Williams stays within the perspective of the speaker, Craig moves over to the side of the hearer to understand their role in communicative exchange.[17] Whether or not confidence is placed in a given testimony depends not only on the accuracy and sincerity of the speaker, as Williams suggests, but on the ability of listeners to detect and respond appropriately to these and other indicators that they are telling the truth. Fricker's research presupposes and to some extent develops a vice-epistemological account of listening, yet without engaging with existing theories of listening. Both testimonial and hermeneutical justices, the two virtues outlined as ways to correct for the epistemic ills described, take place in and through practices and habits of listening, and, in certain passages, Fricker touches on how an agent or members of a collective might learn to listen. And yet the specificity of listening—what might make this aspect of socialization or habit formation distinctive from other perceptual domains, for example—isn't considered. The cultivation of testimonial sensibility is sketched out by analogy with moral formation, the specific sensory, affective, and physiological aspects of aurality set to one side. Hearing or listening is portrayed as one side of a communicative exchange, but why these epistemic vices and virtues should be functions of aurality in particular is not discussed. The ear appears on the scene as little more than the natural dance partner of speech, but would epistemic (in)justice manifest differently if it were a matter of reading and, specifically, reading led by eye rather than readlistening as a critical practice of rhythmically auscultating a text, archive, or speech as a body?

Setting aside what might seem like scruples from a student of sound and listening, let's move onto those features that, for Fricker, distinguish the "virtuous hearer." Such a listener is characterized by a high degree of sensitivity to a speaker's performance. Above all, ears must adopt a posture of "critical openness" that is able to discern true from false and to filter. This isn't just a question of probing the veracity or accuracy of what is said but has a distinctly moral dimension in Fricker's account. This is, to a large degree, because the model of interpersonal communication that Fricker inherits is predicated on trust and the granting and withholding of credibility. She argues that "the feeling of trust in the virtuous hearer is a sophisticated emotional radar for detecting trustworthiness in speakers."[18] It is perhaps telling that Fricker slips from aural to ocular metaphors precisely when the moral dimension comes into view: testimonial sensitivity "allows the virtuous person [NWS: not hearer] to see the world in a certain light" and "virtuous perception gives . . . a view of the world in moral colour."[19] As such, the virtuous ear must be capable of filtering out sincerity from deception or, one might suppose, flattery. This isn't a question of deliberation, though. Unlike those who offer a so-called inferentialist account—one that supposes listeners draw inferences or weigh arguments to assess credibility—Fricker is after something more spontaneous and intuitive. How, though, if achieved without active and time-consuming critical deliberation, can a virtuous hearer accurately assess whether to accord credibility to a speaker and to what is said? The question poses considerable difficulties and will preoccupy Fricker for large stretches of the book. Mindful of the lacunae of non-inferentialist accounts that struggle to identify what kind of rational activity is at play, she seeks an explanation in which the listening at stake is both critical *and* reflexive, without necessarily being reflective.

In many ways, it is this dilemma—of how to explain a reflexive virtuous listening as an exercise of reason—that drives her into the realm of stereotypes and socially situated generalizations, and thus frames the kinds of injustices that she deems to be "core" or embedded into the state of nature. It seems to me, at least, that the struggle to explain how the ear can be discerning, of epistemic as well as moral character, in the absence of a theory of listening beyond the social habituation, is what, to no small degree, commits her to a minimally de-idealizing move.[20] Notwithstanding good intentions, Fricker's is an origin story that admits of minimal contamination at the origin, limited precisely to what may be projected backward from contemporary political configurations and filtered through stereotypical images of human nature drawn from a Eurocentric imperialist canon of political theory and thought in other disciplines, such as the natural sciences or social psychology.

This leads to several problems or unanswered questions, not least that the qualities of listening that qualify as epistemically unjust are limited in scope to perpetuating reductive identity-prejudicial stereotypes and insider/outsider or friend/enemy distinctions—a quintessentially liberal-humanist account of sociopolitical problems. Reducing listening's propensities for injustice to these two categories seems to eschew its multi-fariousness and is far more reductive than the Foucauldian genealogical account of reason's entanglement with power that Fricker half-proffers as a strawman.[21] The problem that confronts Fricker is one that Foucault is well equipped to answer, as Daniele Lorenzini has comprehensively argued: how to distinguish "between what we have a reason to think and what mere relations of power are doing to our thinking" and hence between "rejecting someone's word for good reason and rejecting it out of mere prejudice."[22] Reflecting back on the theoretical underpinnings of her project ten years later, Fricker has observed that, absent such a distinction, the entire notion of epistemic injustice falls down.[23] No one would dispute the value of distinguishing, as Lorenzini elsewhere puts it, "between say, a serious scientific study about the effects of climate change and a tweet by Donald Trump claiming there is no such thing as climate change."[24] And yet it is unclear whether the norms by which one tells good reason from prejudice (Am I justified in rejecting Trump's assertion out of hand or is it because I loathe the man and everything he stands for? Might my prejudice against opportunistic, exploitative, and manipulative purveyors of far-right rhetoric be justified and justification enough?) are suprahistorical. In short, I question whether the ends of justice require rejecting a history—or, more precisely, a genealogy—of reason that is sensitive to the contingencies of history or whether, in fact, the injustice might lie precisely in doing so.

As Lorenzini demonstrates, Foucault is able to locate such a distinction between a norm and the ways in which truth claims have force and take effect in practical action, notwithstanding that such a norm is itself historically contingent.[25] Foucault's interest in the interaction between these two dimensions is also what makes his theory especially productive for understanding the kinds of discerning listening that justice demands. And yet, as I've argued, Foucault, too, is sometimes seduced into attempting to hold open untenable distinctions, such as between truth and rhetoric, in ways that risk flattening the complexity and risk that listening entails. That there might just be no secure way to tell, *by listening*, what is true and what is deception, what is sincere and what is calculated, is what makes listening at once chancy and powerful—or powerful precisely insofar as it is chancy. Recognizing this makes for a much richer theory of listening and its participation in oppression and liberation than Fricker's thin, at bottom metaphorical, conception of "hearer." To understand how material conditions (political-economic, technological, and so on) have forged the ears differently in different times and places, and among different communities, does not reduce it to "a historically situated epiphenomenon of power dynamics in a given society."[26] Likewise, historicizing truth and justice is not relativism. Making a universal out of liberal political theory, on the other hand, does look rather like that.

If listening's viciousness is, on Fricker's account, a supposedly universal and thereby essentialized poison, the same is true of virtuous listening, which is very much an ideal type. I seek in this book to prise apart—*to free*—freedom from purification, from that very freedom from contamination, corruption, noise, criminality, error, and errancy that is the hallmark of the Western metaphysical and liberal political tradition, from a freedom that binds itself in wanting to secure itself from jeopardy. Fricker's project conforms to this trajectory insofar as it wants to purify reason by insisting, as a matter of theoretical principle, if not in practice, on in/justice as a suprahistorical norm grounded in the state of nature and separable from the contingencies of power. Even if her genealogy presupposes a minimally corrupted state of nature, virtuous hearing has a corrective function, in principle capable of restoring, as a matter of second nature, the pure origin that never was. In this way, Fricker is firmly within the horizon of metaphysics with a presupposed ground that has vanished to return as the ideal. Her notion of epistemic justice thus binds listening to idealization and teleology. The truth is in the ears, embedded in an Idea of listening that transcends history. It is this teleological idealization that drives the multiplication of distinctions and discerning judgments that seek to carve up a complex, entangled field of tensions into clear-cut oppositions. The Idea would be lost if it were obtained absolutely (absolute truth, absolute freedom, absolute justice), so the pursuit of the ideal must constantly stop short and hold itself back in injustice and unfreedom to preserve itself as an ideal. It is to that extent that idealization is itself a kind of unfreedom. It binds itself and creates a hall of mirrors to conjure up external constraints.

The consequences of this idealization of virtue and justice are that, for a project that seeks to address silences, it is peculiarly silent on forms of silencing that remain inaudible or are cast as inarticulate noise in the history of logocentrism. The corrective mechanism of virtue is all about restoring the aural counterpart of fallen, mad *phonē* or mere noise to that of idealized, rational *logos*. (To that extent, it is no different from Rancière's redistribution of the sensible.) That is to say, it upholds as the ideal of listening the ear of philosophy as a discipline that constantly negotiates between policing and overflowing its own boundaries, or polices them assiduously because it has already overflowed them. Idealization often appears to be universal, but it actually excludes those who do not conform to the ideal and who may be audible only as mere noisy *phonē*. Both Lorenzini and Dotson, among others such as Ishani Maitra and Rebecca Mason, are able to point to other forms of epistemic justice that do not show up on Fricker's ethical radar, mere hiss at its margins.[27] Indeed, a not inconsiderable portion of the work prompted by Fricker's book has been devoted to expanding or otherwise redrawing the boundaries of epistemic justice.

Both Lorenzini's and Dotson's lacunae concern the capacity for the supposedly virtuous hearer to cultivate a disposition of epistemic humility or questioning toward their own sensitivities and judgments, as well as the bases for their formation and persistence. Put philosophically, they relate to the impossibility of metaphysics hearing its own foundation, for that silence is its condition of possibility. Lorenzini's example (related to that of the irrational *phonē*) is the exclusion altogether from the sphere of rationality of the person deemed "mad" because they either cannot or will not conform to the rules of the game. Not only is their testimony written off in advance as undeserving of credibility; they are also, for that reason, subjected to government power and urged into modes of self-government that conserve and multiply that exclusion. Dotson, for her part, takes issue with the totalizing bent in Fricker's account, specifically that her conception of hermeneutical justice presupposes that there is a single, uniform set of collective hermeneutic resources upon which all hearers draw equally and whose silences must, therefore, be rendered audible and ameliorated.[28] Fricker overlooks the ways in which hegemony blocks the wider circulation of "alternative epistemologies, countermythologies, and hidden transcripts that exist in hermeneutically marginalized communities *among themselves.*" Dotson suggests a third form of injustice—one that perpetuates epistemic oppression. She calls this "contributory" since the hearer's willful hermeneutic ignorance here compounds structural prejudice and marginalization in choosing not to recognize, avail themselves of, or support the flourishing of alterative hermeneutic resources. Within the academy, distortions of others' arguments on account of incompatible hermeneutic resources, whether willfully or otherwise, are a significant obstacle to free inquiry. These cases also illustrate the critical role played by free listening in creating the conditions for academic freedom of expression, in that it insists on the element of responsiveness in scholarly responsibility. Incompatibilities in frameworks of understanding, by contrast, push toward a take-it-or-leave-it stand-off.

Perhaps the takeaway from these examples is not so much the need for a more comprehensive or plural theory as the prosthetic structure of epistemic justice, entailing a series of meta-listenings that keep vigilance over lower levels. If first-order just listening concerns the listener's agential self-vigilance, second-order vigilance as to how prejudice and marginalization operate in structures is itself subject to a higher-order overhearing attuned to the silences in the very resources and frameworks of understanding at work in recognizing second-order structural injustice. There is only an arbitrary end to this regression of listening. If anything, it suggests that there is no final or complete epistemic justice but always in each hearing anew a judgment to be made, a decision to be taken on how to hear, how to speak, how to respond to the other. This is because response-ability is not mine but comes from the other. This is the lesson of the aural metaphors that crop up in our discourse about justice and freedom of expression. Such a model of respons-able listening as a relay that extends and cuts across any outside into the "interior" stands in contrast with the tendency of Fricker's project toward a totalizing account, one that attempts to be comprehensive by delimiting the bounds of its subject and object. This closedness to other forms of silencing is itself, as Dotson observes, a form of epistemic injustice. One of the distinctions into which Fricker is seduced by her idealizing fervor is between culpable forms of epistemic injustice and epistemic "bad luck." The silencing effect of Fricker's conceptual tidiness is especially acute here. Other harms are discounted as "epistemic bad luck" when it is only the absence of relevant conceptual resources for recognizing them as injustice that renders them as theoretical dead zones.

One of the issues may be that Fricker is silent or reticent when it comes to luck or chance. At one point, following Iris Murdoch, she argues that "the morally wisest person remains open to surprises. Or, rather, the fact that she is open-hearted enough to resist the dishonest safety of fixed moral understandings is the crowning mark of her moral wisdom."[29] Moments earlier, echoing Martha Nussbaum, she likened epistemic justice to musical improvisation, and she goes on firmly to deny that epistemic justice is codifiable. And yet, aside from these paeans to openness, and open-endedness, Fricker's hearer remains, in many ways, the paragon of virtue as defined by the canon of moral philosophy, and her account produces a closed, bounded structure that aspires to a conceptual self-sufficiency and forecloses other elaborations. As the hearer refines their virtue through their adaptability in different settings, this begins to feel more like the flexibility by which the neoliberal subject is coerced to govern themself than a radical plasticity that could just as readily blow a hole in the way things are as take the shape of the world.

Notwithstanding the awareness-raising value of Fricker's work, its limitations derive from its desire for theoretical closure and idealization—tendencies that are inimical to the liberation of listening that her clear moral and ethical compass demands. By contrast, for Lorenzini, the possibilizing aspect of Foucauldian genealogy enables normativity to be generated less through an ideal than through the "concrete elaboration and practice of ethico-political counter-conducts, each of which aims to criticize a given regime of truth that still governs (certain aspects of) our conduct."[30] José Medina, meanwhile, theorizes a form of normativity he dubs "guerilla pluralism," which is produced via membership of intersecting and overlapping communities of resistance, rather than any external or transhistorical guiding light.[31] In other words, missing from the canonical account of epistemic injustice is attentiveness to alternative ways of making worlds and concepts. There is in Fricker's theory, for example, an attachment to a selfsame liberal agent, however adaptable, that militates against radical transformation at individual or structural levels.

Some of the experiments in listening for redress and repair whose traces lie in the silences of Western political philosophy may dispense altogether with the notion of credibility and its brutal calculus. They may experiment with other forms of listening, liberated from an ideal, more wayward, more risky—ones that risk undergoing de- and re-subjectification, or abandoning the subject of the subject in favor of collective, solidary attachments and investments. As Dotson suggests, this requires lengthy and dedicated apprenticeships to other forms of listening and being in the world that exceed any conceptual frame already available to them.[32] It also means being prepared to accept the infinite character of the work, and not only in practice. If one can speak of a reparative practice of listening in Black radical or decolonial thought or in the activist spaces of feminist and queer auto-protection, for instance, the repair is of necessity—*and out of justice*—imperfect. Against the will to restore a pure state of nature that ultimately seeks to keep colonial violence in the realm of the unheard, Françoise Vergès observes in the scholarly, artistic, and curatorial practices of Algerian-French visual artist Kader Attia a notion of unfinished repair without erasure.[33] Here the scars and injuries of empire and slavery are left partly healed, partly still wounded in an insistence that the histories of violence be listened to and not be silenced anew in the dissimulating artifice of restoration. Beyond exposing and restoring, it means tearing down institutions of silencing and, in their place, collectively rebuilding, sustaining, maintaining, imperfectly repairing through collective action that transforms those silences and the concepts we use to make sense of them. And no doubt such a leap of faith and imagination in conceptualizing otherwise will make our ears and the genres of our thinking flail.

7

Ears for a Minor Music

The End of Listening

"Yes—I was not—human yesterday."
"Yesterday, they would not have served me,"
    he whispered.
Yesterday, he thought with bitterness, she would
    scarcely have looked at him twice.
"Your people were not my people," she said, "but
    today . . ." He was a man—no more. Yet yesterday . . .

Revisiting W. E. B. Du Bois's speculative fiction a hundred years later, Saidiya Hartman reads "The Comet," which he wrote in the wake of the 1918 pandemic, as the story of a transformation—as an *event*—of listening in and to the world.[1] Hartman refuses to "limn the forces that landed him on the steps of the bank located in the financial district, the predatory heart of the city, and relegated him to the lower depths, as nothing, as nobody . . . arrested on the steps of this cathedral to capitalism, as if it were the crossroads between being a man and being nothing at all." As such, she explains that she chooses to eschew recounting the history of the Black man's negation in "terms *bereft of musicality* [NWS: my emphasis]: accumulation (originary or primitive or recurring), fungibility, natal alienation, kinlessness." Instead, everything hinges, in her palimpsestic retelling of Du Bois's fiction, on the "minor music" made by a "dim, weird radiance that suffused the darkening world" at the moment of its end.[2] Why is it important for Du Bois that, aside from the visual luminescence of the comet, the moment of radical transformation at the end of the world be marked by the sound of music? That the shift should be expressed in what is heard? And then so abruptly be undone by the intrusion of sound? Does the freedom and unfreedom of the Black man really turn so acutely on aurality, and why?

For the seminar that Derrida delivered to unwitting students straight out of high school in 1959–60, scrawled in practically indecipherable handwriting on the back of the second sheet at the end of the paragraph are the words "*New York vide dans mille ans* . . . empty New York in a thousand years. . . ."[3] This is followed by the observation that "silence is what happens when the thunder stops (comment), when sound no longer appears in a certain *space* and *time*." He jots down: "A certain *sensible* quality." But what he said to the students, let alone what they heard in his no doubt perplexing allusions and ellipses, remains unknown, as does why he referred specifically to this scene of New York City in the distant future. I choose, however, to hear his passing reflection as an echo-response, however unintended, to Du Bois's short story—a sonorous event registrable by the senses and rebounding again in Hartman's more recent insistence on musicality. Deconstruction, in this echo, is not completing or providing a crucial theoretical supplement to Black thought. Rather, deconstruction only is on condition that it has already opened its ears to the radicalism that comes from the other. This link I draw is perhaps entirely farfetched considering the quotation from Heidegger scribbled down immediately beforehand that appears to prompt this elliptical reference to an empty New York (though why New York, which surely isn't the noisy city

Heidegger has in mind when discussing an obscure saying of Heraclitus about listening to the *logos*?). The background to the Heidegger passage cited by Derrida might even be illuminating for understanding the exclusion temporarily alleviated in Du Bois's story and for reckoning with the nexus between listening and freedom.

The Heraclitan saying of which Heidegger has been trying to make sense begins with a question enjoining the listener not to listen to me (to the human audible voice of Heraclitus) but to the *logos* (a nonhuman, inaudible or at least soundless voice).[4] At stake, then, is an aural discrimination between the human and what is somehow other than human. Heidegger speculates that this listening to the *logos* consists in a mode of attending-to that goes beyond auditory perception (mere hearing) and is better described as "hearkening (*hörchen*)."[5] This hearkening is a uniquely human capacity. Listening to a world to which one already belongs is "freedom itself" and, specifically, the freedom proper to the human who alone is capable of being open to the open. It is paradoxically a kind of obedience (*gehorchen*), though nothing like subjugation, apparently. This "authentic" listening is not absent from other kinds of listening, such as sensory perception, but as it were keeps silent within them insofar as it is forgotten. This leads to a topsy-turvy conclusion for Heidegger: the authentic, spiritual hearkening is a metaphorical derivation of acoustic hearing rather than an originary ground that has gone to ground. By contrast, Heidegger believes that, far from hearing because we have ears, humans have, and can have, ears *because they hear*, because they already belong, inescapably, to a world in which noise is possible. At this point, tracking Heidegger's text, Derrida notes the direct quotation: "We humans are able to listen to the thunder of the heavens, to the rustling of the woods, to the flowing of a spring, to the tones of the harp, to the clattering of motors, and to the noise of the city—insofar as we belong, or do not belong, to all of this."[6] Heidegger then goes on to distinguish between listening to "the colossal noise that the human is now causing upon earth's battered surface" and hearkening to the "song of the earth (*Lied des Erdes*)" that is untouched by all this noise.

Let us return now to Hartman's reading of Du Bois's story and her tuning in to that little phrase "minor music," bearing in mind how Heidegger maps the boundaries of humanity onto different listening capacities and different objects of aural attention. Du Bois's protagonist is a Black man who is sent down to the dangerous lower vaults of the banks where he works, banished to another capitalist space of Black confinement, a picture of the commodity at once in circulation and enclosure. Held among the loot and disavowed secrets of empire, this not-quite-human man is scarcely noticed. He is "outside the world." Only with the silencing of the city by the comet's mass extinction event, and thus only at the end of the world, can he become human, both in his own eyes and in the eyes of the only other survivor, an affluent white woman. For a moment the gaping difference between them is given a reprieve, they become primal Man and Woman, and the possibility emerges of interracial love and fruitful generation. He is human and he is free. Hartman glosses this moment of radiance as a fascinated silence in which the man's shackles "seemed to rattle and fall from his soul," explicitly referencing the liberation of resonance: "The minor music, the sonorous echo of earth released from the order of men, resonates in the leveled city, announcing this new state of relation inaugurated by the apocalypse, a state in which blackness is no longer relegated to nothing and death. Catastrophe produces this vast romance, as if ruin is the prerequisite for interracial love, as if the enclosure of blackness could only be breached and caste abolished by the destruction of the world."

Was this the moment, the justice, that Derrida was somehow

imagining when he thought of New York empty of noise a millennium into the future? In any event, sound is not incidental—to Derrida's understanding of responsibility or to Hartman's reading of Du Bois and the possibility of Black futures. In "The Comet" the moment of hope, of relief, of freedom, and of a certain sensible attunement, is rudely broken by the "honk! honk!" of a motor, the "clang—crash—clang!" of urban noise restored, with the "roar and ring" of elevators and the "murmur and babel of voices." We are back to the world from which, Derrida underscores, there is no escaping. If for Heidegger it is the delimiting mark of the human to be able to listen to the song of the earth, for Hartman it is only with the liberation of Earth's sonorousness from the human order and from the human ear's opening to the world that Black freedom is possible, even thinkable. This minor music is the sound of the end of the human ear and a listening that imprisons Black people in a world from which they are systematically excluded. The ending of the story—with the restoration of urban noise and of the order of white supremacy, with the reuniting of the man with the mother of his child, whom she carries dead in her arms—reminds us that this is a stillborn hope. Escape remains impossible even in fugitivity, reflects Hartman. "Even when on the run and in flight," condemnation is permanently affixed to enslaved peoples and their descendants by a stigmatizing name, "a brutal address," thereby stressing the aural character of the violence as well as the fragile possibility of transfiguration.

Hartman dubs the story a "satire of failed democracy," exposing how "the stranglehold of white supremacy appears so unconquerable, so eternal that its only certain defeat is the end of the world, the death of Man." War and human rights having proved insufficient, only environmental catastrophe can undo the color line and its calculus of life and death, allowing the enslaved to be counted as human. "The paradox," she continues, "is that human extinction provides the answer and the corrective to the modern project of whiteness, which Du Bois defines as *the ownership of the earth forever and ever*, the possessive claim of the universe itself." We are a world away from Fricker's self-correcting virtuous hearer and in a space where only the radical demolition of the liberal property regime, and the edifice of European metaphysics that upholds it, can open up the space for creating new ways of listening and being in the world. I read Hartman's intervention as a rejoinder to Heidegger's reading of Heraclitus, prying apart the capaciousness of living from its reduction to the *logos*. At the heart of such an abolitionist project to free listening would be a twin effort to dismantle all the ways in which *listening is fixed* and, at the same time, all the ways in which not simply are certain bodies and certain ears excluded from human exceptionalism but *the human is fixed by reference to delimited genres of listening*. To undo this entangled twin strategy of ontologically privileging (over the non- or inhuman) and determining (by reference to a proper essence or teleological production) will mean freeing listening from not merely existing but all horizons of humanism.

Sylvia Wynter's critique of the overrepresentation of the Greco-Roman cum Judeo-Christian bourgeois conception of the human—one that is defined by possession of (and hence, I'd note, the capacity to listen to) the *logos*—underscores the intimacy between the human/not-quite-human/non-human hierarchy and the supposed ordering of the world and of the cosmos.[7] In the early seminar Derrida, for his part, does not make many notes, aside from the reference to Heidegger, about the relation between silence and world, but the idea of space does figure strongly in those pages. Whence the significance of the noisy or silenced city as a space in which the political order finds its spatial extension, whether with the exclusion in ancient Greece of women and slaves from the *polis* or with color lines in cities of the Global North today. One of the frames that limits the modalities of listening available to us today is an anthropocentric and humanistic conception of the space in which we listen and live, and hence our relation to the world around us. According to the Western bourgeois (settler-)colonial tradition, in which the entire universe revolves around the *logos*, Indigenous and African peoples in particular are sub- or irrational *and* incapable of relationality.[8] This claim is used to justify missionary "civilization" and imperialist expropriation. Such a world order, premised on a notion of what constitutes a properly human listening and a listening proper to the human, has pushed to the margins other genres of being human and of what I will describe as *ecological attunement*.

This listening ecologically is to be distinguished from a listening primarily to the voice and to discrete sounds, as envisaged in Heidegger's discussion of hearing. If for Heidegger, the human is uniquely capable of hearkening to the song of earth and, as Derrida observes in a later interview, uniquely capable of keeping quiet, rather than simply mute, it is not simply a question of expanding the definition of the human, thereby assimilating other genres of being and listening into the hegemonic categories of Eurocentric thought.[9] As Kathryn Yusoff writes: "The move *toward* a more expansive notion of humanity must be made with care. It cannot be based on the presupposition that emancipation is possible once the racial others and their voices are included finally to realize this universality, but must be based on the recognition that these 'Others' are already inscripted in the foundation formulation of the universal *as a space of privileged subjectification*."[10]

Black and Brown bodies, especially women's bodies, are typically cast as the unheard, unseen, disposable lives who, as Françoise Vergès reminds us, dispose of the increasing piles of waste produced by racialized capitalism, which nonetheless demands glacially clean surfaces of circulation: office buildings, luxury hotels, white-walled galleries around urban centers of global finance.[11] These silenced workers of color who clean and care for the white bourgeoisie are as erased as the waste that they are expected to clean up. Their inaudibility is possible, to no small degree, because of the exclusion of certain forms of life that do not meet certain ideals of cognition, sociality, and aesthesis elevated into a universal so as to justify and at the same time silence that foundational exclusion. To eschew calls for revised—read, more inclusive—foundations of the human isn't necessarily to embrace Afropessimism. Humanism, of whatever stripe, determines the human by reference to inalienable features said to be "proper" and as the object of its own teleological production, even if that object is (in the hands of someone like Jean-Luc Nancy) to efface itself, to dispossess itself of any essence, to be improper. The continuity with chattel slavery lies in conceiving of humanity as "property," if only as the property of sovereign self-possession.

Such humanist reductions are closely related to the tendency of white bourgeois listening to render Black and Brown bodies inaudible, because it reduces itself to a particular genre of listening at the expense of others: a listening attuned only to what lies ahead and to hand; to what represents the possibility of instrumentalization and the relentless path of progress, productivity, and profit; to what may be taken in hand, appropriated, possessed (and then thrown aside in the onward march); and to what may be foreseen. For this listening, the world is severely cut down and dug out. It exists only within a narrow opening through which all value may be extracted, all resources siphoned off. It is a small step from Heidegger's romanticized song of the earth to the siren song of fossil fuels still in the ground, ravages and plunder laying waste to sacred lands and stripping bare the riches of the earth, a glint (or cartoonish dollar sign) in the eye of the oil executive and the social-democratic politicians in government too cowardly to hear otherwise. This is a listening too craven to listen to the sounds of Indigenous reason and forms of testimony that confound Western-liberal ears, to the voices of the young people and the poor terrified for their futures, whose silence at the ballot box sounds more loudly only insofar as it will go unheard and so may be safely ignored, and to the earth and creaturely life being driven to extinction.

Five years ago a call for papers for a special issue of the *Oxford Literary Review*, devoted to the theme of "ext: writing extinction," pricked up my ears even if I did not directly respond to it. The call prompted a thought experiment that has weighed on me and that ought to be taken up seriously: *What will remain of listening after the event of human extinction?* And what would this unheard-of discourse on extinction, a discourse on the extinction of human listening, at present still relatively marginal to the discussion of this catastrophe, have to contribute to our understanding of ecological destruction and to ways of living on in the face of this impending doom, at once looming and out of earshot and hence silenced. Over the last few years, I have pondered what it would mean to take seriously the possibility of the end of human listening and how, by projecting ourselves into such a future, we might be compelled to listen otherwise in the present. For me, this is one of the things that Hartman's reading of Du Bois's short story brings to the fore when her ears prick up at his word "music," described as "minor" since the radicality of the change—the dismantling and rebuilding—that it represents is so fragile, the hope so short-lived, as to be almost unheard amid the din of the capitalist world. If Hartman does not directly ask after the genre and generation of listening after extinction, she does find in Du Bois an answer of sorts to the question: What would the end of the world sound like? From here, it becomes imperative to ask what ears would be needed to hear this sound of the end of the world, if they can no longer be human ears—ears for a minor music.

There is a reason why Derrida, *contra* Heidegger, repeatedly notes and underlines the words "in time" and "in space" in the manuscript for the seminar on silence. The two are key to the destructive consequences of the logocentric consequences of listening. If empire is in part a fantasy about what could be heard, discovered, collected, expropriated at the ends of the earth in spatial terms, this fantasy is inseparable from a *temporal* conception of "end." Listening after extinction would draw a diagonal line from the reduction of aural spatiality to the radical finality of the impact of imperialist extractivism at the intersection of climate catastrophe, environmental destruction, and species extinction. If listening is a form of *extending* an ear—as the French *tendre l'oreille* suggests far more than the metaphor of debt in the English *lend an ear*, which still fixates on that Christian-capitalist nexus of faith, debt, and usury—there arises the question of how the ear *tenses* the end of the world. By this I mean how the ears place the world and the environment around them under a particular tension through a certain ex-tension of the aural faculty. I am far from the first to suggest that the Anthropocene expresses itself in a grammatical tense in French called the *futur antérieur*. This future is not simply what is going to happen. Rather, the tense marks a vantage point in the future from which it will be possible to look back and assess what has happened by then. The Anthropocene is a function of geological time; the change it transcribes can become legible only after it has happened. And yet we can anticipate it. The anthropogenic destruction is what *will have* come to pass.

Geological time focuses minds, in the work of Dipesh Chakrabarty, for example, on the event of universal human extinction as the source of the Anthropocene's aporetic tensing, the event from which Du Bois's survivors are uniquely spared.[12] Du Bois's story is in the realm of speculative fiction because there is logically an impossibility in perceiving extinction itself and hence in hearing the end of the world as such. Who would be alive to hear after life? By the time extinction becomes audible in the present (if that were possible), the human, animal, and other organic auralities capable of hearing it *will have been* already rendered extinct. Listening to the end of the world is thus tensed in the *futur antérieur*, asking us to stretch out our ears into a future phenomenological horizon from which to listen back to an event, still in the future from our present today, to a traumatic memory that will already have happened and will have thereby rendered that horizon impossible. This is a listening before which listening, at least in its human and organic forms, will have been over. Du Bois answers the dilemma by presenting fleetingly the unimaginable possibility of Black life liberated. His speculative fiction, despite its vivid present tense (the minor music "resonates," the catastrophe "produces"), is secretly in the *futur antérieur*. When he says Blackness "is no longer relegated to nothing," he means "when it *will no longer have been* relegated." And the condition of the "as if" names a possibility foreseeable only insofar as it will already be behind, past, long gone: "as if the enclosure of blackness *will only have been breached* and caste *will only have been abolished* by the destruction of the world."[13]

In his 2019 article responding to the *Oxford Literary Review* call for papers, Philippe Lynes leaps directly off from the "ext" of extension: "The future anterior temporality of extinction designates a trauma just before our feet, but one that seemingly can only be accounted for once its threshold—the limit where writing ceases—is crossed."[14] Lynes's formulation is spatial, a threshold drawn like a line in the sand, but the temporal insinuates itself in spatial metaphor. "*Before* our feet," he says to refer to what comes in advance, to what temporally precedes the progress of the human animal that walks on two feet, so-called *homo erectus* who, in standing upright, now not only has the world spatially before, *in front of*, himself and hence amenable to the instrumental grasp of his hand but, moreover, enters into a temporal horizon of *fore*sight and the calculable anticipation. The world becomes for him what it *might be*, the homophony of power and sovereign authority in English here being no coincidence. This story of the event of humankind makes him the author of what he may, in the jussive subjunctive mode, let be, or order or wish it so—*Listen! Let them listen!*

And yet, as I have explored elsewhere, humanity can only listen *forward* since in the history of evolution there was, coextensive with the changes in the cervical spine that gave rise to the upright stance, a loss of the species' capacity to turn its ears backward.[15] Even though most other mammals still retain this capacity (think of how a cat's ears move when they detect a sound behind them), the human is in the position of being able to look forward only at the expense of turning its back on what is behind it. Human extinction is perceptible to human ears provided that they turn away from—turn their backs on— the event of extinction as such. Once the event of extinction looming from behind pricks up the ear, humanity, like Orpheus, will already have been condemned to death. Humanism is thus predicated on an aporia, on forgetting, disavowing, silencing the traumatic destruction it will have wrought even on itself. David Wills describes the modality of the *futur antérieur* in his book on the death penalty as "what appeared to be happening within the perspective of its own future gets preempted by the past."[16] This means that the *futur antérieur* does not merely capture the perfectedness or irreparability of the past event, as in this kind of formulation: "By the time extinction becomes audible [and French will phrase this as 'will have become audible'] (human) listening will already be extinct." Rather, it also speaks to the reopening of the finite brought about by an undecidable, contingent relation between already-happened and yet-to-come: "As soon as (human) listening is extinct ['will have become extinct'], extinction can be heard." Listening is not simply impossible after extinction. *Listening is possible only once it is impossible.*

Rather than a virtue that a subject has or might have at hand to acquire, cultivate, and make use of, the listening I have in mind is shot through by the dimension of the impossible and the incalculable—what can only surprise the ears from behind. It has many of the qualities that Wills finds in a dorsal listening, or listening from behind, whereby listening is not something that a subject can grasp, or that can even fall incident to a subject, but what will always already have prostheticized, technologized, animated the ears from behind in a movement of de- and re-subjectivating them.[17] Listening after extension entails a form of temporal and spatial extension that radicalizes the extension of perception at the edge with/of the world in Freud's phrase: "Psyche is extended; knows nothing of it." The genre of listening that has been repressed in logocentrism is listening as unconscious extension, the entire apparatus of the ear as a secret prosthesis reaching out and deeply interconnected with the world in ec(h)ological fashion. To imagine listening after/to extinction points to this prostheticity in that it invites appeals to the modalities of listening experimented with by posthuman or even postorganic life, or in experiences of technologically mediated survival—to what Wills calls "inanimation."[18] Such listening is palpably prosthetic in that it relies upon a technological or postorganic extension of aural reach, of the projective capacity of the ear beyond its horizon of predictable foresight. It is out of surveilling earshot as much as out of reach of the grasping fist. Attention to this prostheticity, spatially and temporally, also reveals that all listening comes from or via the other as a series of articulations relayed from outside right into the ostensible presence and present of our interiority and self-identical simultaneity. It thus dismantles the edifice of the metaphysical (self-)possessing subject of bourgeois liberalism.

The question is how to rebuild listening from this point, how to spark the invention of and experimentation with new genres, forms, and modalities of listening. To start with, this means going beyond the horizon of humanism to understand practices and ideas of listening outside this dominant frame of reference. For Heidegger, the definition of the rational animal, as an organism that has or can listen to *logos*, is ultimately complicit with biologism and is insufficiently humanistic. Derrida, however, rejects the Heideggerian idea that only man has a world, can listen to this world, and is capable of keeping silent in response, and that the animal and nonorganic entities are without world and listening, simply mute in an experience of immediate contact with their environment. If free speech depends for its liberty on how it is received and hence on listening as its condition of possibility, such listening must be liberated from the concepts and templates that fix it. These determinations of how and what the ears hear must give way to more capacious understandings that allow freedom of expression to be an occasion for a radical transformation of how the listener listens, thinks, and acts in the world. These means open up to forms of justice and projects of betterment that exist outside the canon of moral and political philosophy in the West, in which such lofty goals are predicated on moving beyond and setting aside more base, "beastly" instincts.

Animals practice listening in ways that unsettle the directive, teleological, instrumentalizing, and assimilative hunger of the liberal-humanist subject. *Undrowned*, by queer Black scholar and activist Alexis Pauline Gumbs, is a remarkable testament to tuning into such aural possibilities in animal lives as she transforms her human ear by detour through the reverberant intergenerational aural practices of marine mammals. In some ways, the modalities of listening that Gumbs explores strike me as a posthuman transformation of the technologies of ocean tomography that have been used to monitor ocean temperatures and, hence, to chart the devastating progress of climate change, as well as to round out accounts of impacts on the biodiversity and health of underwater ecosystems. David Palumbo-Liu observes, in an unflinching account of recovering the audibility of minority voices, that when speech emanates from the wrong place, when someone speaks without "knowing their place," they are chastised and silenced.[19] Palumbo-Liu argues compellingly that, conversely, we must make shared spaces in which these voices sound and are heard. In Gumbs's account, listening is more transformative and revolutionary in its "quietening down and tuning in" than in showing up and speaking up.[20] Hers is less about being included as meaningful in the domain of audible voices, as Palumbo-Liu's Rancièran account tends to suggest, even as he champions alternative spaces of solidarity and resistance, echoing Du Bois's reconstructionist thinking. Gumbs is more interested in how listening itself might be transformed by opening her ears up to learning from the sociality and care of other species and in listening *with* them.

Such lessons promise transformation by remaking, among other things, the spatial dimension of listening. Gumbs is particularly interested in the practice of echolocation used by marine mammals, which is threatened by noise pollution in oceans and rising temperatures due to anthropogenic climate change. Echolocation is not only or even mostly a matter of communication; it is ecological, taking the measure of one's surroundings. Describing herself as a "marine mammal apprentice," Gumbs puts queer Black liberation at the centre of her meditations, listening across species that struggle to survive the militarized extractivism that empire has wrought on the planet and its creatures. As the oceans darken and cloud over with the blood spilled by the transatlantic slave trade, there is nothing left but to bounce the sound off one's environment and listen in relation to what returns or what shatters in sonic shards, dispersed in the water. Such ecological listening refuses to submit difference to identification, exclusion, pity, or sadistic enjoyment.

Deconstructionist philosopher of listening Peter Szendy has also been drawn to the idea of animal echolocation (in bats) as a way to overcome fixing the ear to a single point or listening to a single ear, shifting instead to what happens in the "interaural difference" between the two ears.[21] In other words, difference can be unsettling and resist settling on a single conception of the world around us. Gumbs isn't concerned only with the differantial character of listening but with what I am calling the specifically ecological—or, maybe better, ec(h)olocatory— dimension of sound and listening in motion. Echolocation, which requires an at least binary system of aural perception, is always multiple but also indirect and dispersive. Its reflections allow it to navigate around objects. It is not a simple matter of negation or inversion but of multiple reflections and cir-cumnavigation. Undoing enslavement and subjection is less a matter of a head-on assault or of overturning metaphysical, humanist listening than it is of turning *around*—and specifi-cally turning the ears around, like our cats do—to overturn the ways that have affixed humanity's ears, like its gaze, to the front and to the mastery, control, and ultimately the destruction of the world. Gumbs's book is at turns tender and militant, and also a work of mourning that relies on strategies akin to Hart-man's critical fabulation, creating resonances in the blanks and silences of historical and contemporary empirical records. Her experiments with listening like and with marine mammals create ears that will have heard the lost and forgotten. As such, anticipatory echolocation points toward prosthetic, differantial, and temporally and spatially disjointed genres of listening that need to be nurtured to combat—in the present—the ravages of imperialist extraction.

Ec(h)olocatory listening disrupts the possibility for gathering listening into a universal account or, indeed, for a listening that gathers what it hears according to a totalizing notion of the universal. Derrida lambasts the modern humanitarianism that has arisen out of a humanist conception of man as a "dishonest fiction," borrowing and repurposing the syntagm from Carl Schmitt.[22] For Schmitt what is *schrecklick* (fearsome or terrible) is "not only treating men as beasts, but the hypocrisy of an imperialism that gives itself the alibi of universal humanitarianism (therefore beyond the sovereignty of a nation-state) in order in fact to protect or extend the powers of a particular nation-state." Derrida glosses this critique of the universal discourse of man by arguing that imperialism is hypocritical for combating its enemies in the name of human rights while treating them "like beasts, like non-men, or like outlaws, like werewolves"; far from waging war, in "what would today be called a state terrorism that does not speak its name," "it is itself behaving like a werewolf." Derrida, like Schmitt, rejects this alibi as a depoliticization of the state, but at that point he sharply parts ways with the theorist of enmity, accusing him of remaining confined within the frame of humanistic moralism, among other criticisms. If Schmitt denounces imperialism with a human face as a hypocritical ruse for failing to declare war openly (it does not speak freely), Derrida instead aims at "a *slow and differentiated* deconstruction" of the dominant logic of nation-state sovereignty, to make way for "an other politicization, a repoliticization that does not fall into the same ruts of the 'dishonest fiction,' . . . and therefore another concept of the political."[23] To free listening—and speech with it—means seeking out this other concept of the political, this repoliticization by other means and listening's role in it.

Listening might just get away from me. I might not be able to pin it down. I have discussed two examples of multiple and out-of-joint auralities that create alternative futures that *might have been* and thus resist extractivist, biopolitical, and racializing modalities of listening. To try, though, to catalog, enumerate, define the ways in which listening escapes its logo- and Eurocentric fixation would itself risk becoming a kind of "hungry listening," cannibalistic in its desire to devour, appropriate, put in the white liberal's pocket as if a souvenir of Black and Indigenous life.[24] It is a truism that white-liberal paeans to progressive politics often end with calls and appeals, searching for others to bring their vision for a better future. Leaving listening as a demand on the other, rather than receiving it as a gift from the other, is something I want to try to resist. As such I want to name a few more gratefully received gifts, words that have whispered or percussed their way into my ears and swirled and hammered around in their spirals, unsettling the equilibrium of their boundary policing between left and right.

Am I about to commit a genre flail? A genuine act of provocation is more than "the empty rhetorical gesture of the contrarian," the blurb for this series informs me; it should "intervene in the present by invoking an as yet undecided future radically different from what is declared to be possible in the present and, in so doing, to arouse the desire for bringing about change."[25] How should one begin to wind down in "the genres of the manifesto, the polemical essay, the intervention, and the pamphlet" if not with a rallying cry to action? After all the bold exhortations—above all: free listening!—all I can offer by way of sketching out that groping way forward to a different future is a descant to a minor music.

The genre flail—the notion comes from Lauren Berlant, an author known for their brilliant fraying and remaking of genres of writing—isn't something one aspires to or sets out to achieve.[26] It isn't the end point of some moral, ethical, or political project, like a virtue to be cultivated or a possibility to be realized. The flailing isn't so much anti-teleological as it undoes the very possibility of ends, ideals, and totalities from the get-go. The exemplary case of genre flailing for Berlant happens in response to a crisis "so that we don't fall through the cracks of knowledge and noise into suicide or psychosis."[27] Listening is very much bound up with genre flailing, I would suggest, even if it isn't something Berlant expressly considers. This is because it is a response to a disturbance in the attachment to one's objects, and not limited to the usual ambivalence about their transforming. "We improvise 'like crazy,'" suggests Berlant, "after an object, or object world, becomes disturbed in a way that intrudes on one's confidence about how to move in it." I might flail, but I am not capable as such of a genre flail; it is something that comes from the outside, from the other, that alters my object—deconstruction, say, or Black radical thought—so as to disturb the security of my investment and attachment. Such flailing, as the etymology of the word suggests, is more like an experience of whiplash that dislodges all my formulas, habits, assurances, genres of thinking, writing, listening, being that stabilize something like "me."

Listening is a primary way of forming attachments, and not just to the maternal voice and all the umbilical power of genesis, generativity, and generational inheritance embedded in that aural attachment. I am suggesting that we think of the radical transformation and liberation of listening less as a project that we collectively might master than as something that will require and proceed from our genres of listening being put into flail and flight. The genre flailing that ensues might not be the brilliant demonstration of inventive improvisatory power that Nussbaum imagines of the virtuous moral agent. It might just be the experiments we make with our ears when accustomed ways of listening to the world around us no longer work or satisfy and we have to get by without falling back on them. Or we might even be "fabulously unimaginative," throwing "prefab frames," "common sense," "litanies of things to do," and performative rituals of protest and accusation. As the faith that citizens in rich Western democracies have historically put in political leaders to listen to them and represent them has been profoundly shaken, this crisis of listening has seen plenty resorting to strategies and methods with little prospect of success in the charged anger of the post-Trumpian world (polling, focus groups, listening tours).

Berlant's examples of things we might do when we flail lean more to the side of speech ("throwing language and gesture and policy and interpretation"), but—and perhaps this is flailing on my part—I'm more intrigued to think about what happens when we let listening flail, when it doesn't know where our ears should turn or be directed, or in which orientation, when the things that used to prick up our ears no longer register, when other sounds intrude into the aural world we've carefully constructed as a space of safety, when the mere fact of being asked to listen to someone or something scrambles all our moral and political coordinates, when our possible range of responses has pulled the rug from under our feet. These are the kinds of experiences that promise to shake up and liberate expression and the hearing that marginalized voices get or don't. Their capacity for correction and redress is uncertain, yet charged, veering between hopelessness and passionate conviction about what can be achieved when we put our ears to it in new ways. Whether genre flailing is a "big suck of our best creative energy" I'm not so sure; it might just be the way in which we feel our way along and together to another way of listening and living in the world without feeling we can master it. When our genres of listening flail, it might well be that they are both destructive and reconstructive in the sense of abolition democracy. So if I argue that freeing listening is an abolitionist endeavor, as Berlant puts it, "whenever one is destroying some things in the object one is also trying to protect something else in it that matters, that deserves a better world for its circulation, or that constitutes a crucial anchor."[28]

Sometimes, though, going AWOL is a more purposeful strategy, improvised in a crisis, yet not without a certain cunning or calculation. Vergès has written about the "art of marooning" practiced by slaves on the island of La Réunion, where she spent some of her childhood and adolescence.[29] Marronage consisted in enslaved people running away, perhaps for an hour, a day or several, or even years, and building alternative spaces of community in the mountains away from the unfreedom of the colonial plantations. They even rejected the names by which the slaveowners had commodified them to name themselves anew in their own tongue. In a leap of imagination that was formative for Vergès growing up, "they carved a land that belied the normalization of enslavement." The maroons' temporary escape and living otherwise, however briefly, bequeaths a lesson to history, and we might well wonder if it provides a template for temporary reprieves from our captive genres of listening. And yet in a manifesto written with a group of young artists of color, as part of a workshop that Vergès held in 2017 in Paris, they issue the following words of caution, worth quoting at length to underscore the persistence of disruption that is needed to free listening:

> Making a reified icon of the Maroon would be to betray their memory. It is a danger that looms for all figures of freedom and, before we know it, we would risk seeing this figure set in stone on the fronts of museums. We take our imperative of constantly being on the move, in motion, inventing new, free territories, from the Maroons. The night welcomes our dreams and opens up still unexplored paths. We claim the right to be unfinished and contradictory. We want to creatively redefine the visual traces of history, to explore the past to analyze the present and imagine the future. Our utopia must remain a never-achieved goal; it must instill a permanent state of curiosity.[30]

This can also entail reimagining existing experiences and habits that bear the marks of brutal oppression. Elsewhere Vergès refers to Harriet Jacobs's "loophole of retreat."[31] For years after her escape Jacobs would be hidden away in the tiny garret of her grandmother's shed, accessible only by a concealed trap door carved meticulously by her carpenter uncle. It is hard to imagine a space more emblematic of the crawlspace, the space of confinement, the quarantine imposed by the threat of violence, but this space of enclosure was also, for Jacobs, transformed into room for practices of freedom—imagining, thinking, writing, no doubt listening from her concealed position. In this way I would suggest that freeing listening calls for inhabiting, dismantling, yet also repurposing and reimagining the institutions of listening (the school classroom, the lecture theatre, the radio, the Houses of Parliament, Speaker's Corner, and so on) so as to unsettle the veneer of democracy.

Among other things, this listening would not need to hear

all, to make everything audible and subject to examination or any other response. This doesn't contradict the critical impulse that is a necessary part of free academic inquiry and democratic scrutiny. It just says that amenability to critique is an expression of infinite curiosity rather than the desire to close things down in judgment or to "cling on tighter to one's way of [hearing] the world."[32] Just as I have suggested listening might escape me, some sounds, some voices, or some utterances might escape these ears in retreat, out of a curiosity that does not need to know *everything* (which would be the end of curiosity) and out of respect and care, as Anne Dufourmantelle has suggested, for the secret garden of the other, and of my own, in which an inner life of freedom might blossom.[33] We imagine that true, frank speech comes from the depths of the soul, encrypted in the unconscious; it is also what we want to possess in the other. All this is perhaps, we suspect, that there may be some dissimulation that we want to expose. Those kinds of secrets keep you, imprison you. Instead of an interdiction bound to fuel obsession, "wisdom would mean turning around, diverting yourself—better to cultivate your own garden, invite the other to lose themselves in it, for nothing is as powerful as an invitation into yourself to heal the desire to break into the other."

Listening too might veil and sequester itself in a kind of aural opacity. This would not be to surveil from an undetected position of power but, in an aural counterpart to the refusal to speak that can speak the language of resistance more loudly than a thousand manifestos, it might mean distracting power and dodging violence by appearing not to listen (and more radically than Hobbesian civil discretion, whose aim is not to disturb unduly the social order). Vergès describes the enslaved domestic worker, standing silently while washing, dressing and undressing her owner, who "pretended not to listen while collecting facts."[34] This is listening as a loophole of retreat that creates a form of freedom by veiling one's listening. Alternatively, this could be a listening that conceals itself because it knows that hearing as much as possible is not as important as making room for testimony judiciously. While we are frequently urged in leadership workshops and the like to cultivate active listening as a virtue that will solicit more testimony and make the other feel heard, there are also times when, out of justice and out of service for the truth, listening should retreat so as not to press or hang so heavily as to induce reticence or to avoid giving the impression that it would snatch the words straight out of the speaker's mouth. Listening might shrewdly withdraw precisely so as to allow speech to unfold. The ears need not always be wide open to listening, expressing, and understanding the world. What we mean by "feeling heard" isn't necessarily the license to tell all, for that might shut off the transformation of silence and repressed ghosts. Listening instead might be *gentle*, so that it "comes to rest in the interstices of cruelty and turns them inside out like a glove."[35]

Freedom of expression can, of course, be exercised to tell, persuade, convince, challenge. It becomes all the more powerful, though, when it is understood as a much more capacious set of demands, invitations, and exhortations to undergo transformation within the individual psyche but also in the remaking of social infrastructures. There is undoubtedly a bridle in our universities and our public forums on expression of dissent from those excluded from power and marginalized from social norms and universals. But if some decry "cancel culture" (often while continuing to enjoy the platform of power), I retort "abolition culture." This means dismantling the institutions, structures, practices, norms, and contracts of listening that perpetuate and justify existing forms of oppression and inequality via distributions of audibility. In their place, as Du Bois describes in *Black Reconstruction*, we need the incalculable promise of creating, experimenting with, happening upon, muddling through together with new and transformed genres of listening that are guided by the promise of an equal being-together-in-the-world. Talk and action alone will not get us there. Freedom will only be the inheritance and secret garden of all when we free listening.

NOTES

SILENCING LISTENING

1. Butt v. Secretary of State for the Home Department, [2019] EWCA Civ 933, 171–72.

2. J. L. Austin, *How to Do Things with Words: The William James Lectures Delivered at Harvard University in 1955*, ed. J. O. Urmson and M. Sbisà (Oxford: Oxford University Press, 1975 [1965]).

3. Austin, *How to Do Things with Words*, 116–17.

4. Mary C. Scudder, *Beyond Empathy and Inclusion: The Challenge of Listening in Democratic Deliberation* (New York: Oxford University Press, 2020).

5. Scudder, *Beyond Empathy*, 107–8.

6. Guy Longworth, "Illocution and Understanding," *Inquiry: An Interdisciplinary Journal of Philosophy* (2019), DOI: 10.1080/0020174X.2019.1667869.

7. Stanley Cavell, *Philosophy the Day After Tomorrow* (Cambridge MA: Harvard University Press, 2005), 172.

8. Longworth, "Illocution."

9. Daniele Lorenzini, "From Recognition to Acknowledgement: Rethinking the Perlocutionary," *Inquiry: An Interdisciplinary Journal of Philosophy* (2020), DOI: 10.1080/0020174X.2020.1712231.

10. See, for example, Alessandra Tanesini, "'Calm Down Dear': Intellectual Arrogance, Silencing and Ignorance," *Proceedings of the Aristotelian Society*, supplementary volume 90 (2016): 71–92. See also Miranda Fricker's work on testimonial injustice, including

"Silence and Institutional Prejudice," in *Out from the Shadows: Analytical Feminist Contributions to Traditional Philosophy*, ed. Sharon L. Crasnow and Anita M. Superson (New York: Oxford University Press, 2012), 287–306.

11. Alexander Bird, "Illocutionary Silencing," *Pacific Philosophical Quarterly* 83 (2002): 1–15.

12. Saidiya Hartman, *Wayward Lives, Beautiful Experiments: Intimate Histories of Riotous Black Girls, Troublesome Women and Queer Radicals* (New York: Norton, 2019).

13. Christina Sharpe, *In the Wake: On Blackness and Being* (Durham NC: Duke University Press, 2016).

14. David Wills, *Dorsality: Thinking Back Through Technology and Politics* (Minneapolis: University of Minnesota Press, 2008). See also "Positive Feedback: Listening Behind Hearing," in *Thresholds of Listening: Sound, Technics, Space*, ed. Sander van Maas (New York: Fordham University Press, 2015), 70–88.

15. Jean-Luc Nancy, "The Inoperative Community," trans. Peter Connor, in *The Inoperative Community* (Minneapolis: University of Minnesota Press, 1991), 4.

16. W. E. B. Du Bois, *Black Reconstruction in America, 1860–1880* (New York: The Free Press, 1998 [1935]); Angela Davis, *Abolition Democracy: Beyond Prison, Torture, and Empire* (New York: Seven Stories Press, 2005).

THE MARGINS OF LIBERTY

1. John Stuart Mill, *On Liberty* (Cambridge: Cambridge University Press, 2011), 22.

2. Mill, *On Liberty*, 96.

3. Mill, *On Liberty*, 13, 12.

4. Quassim Cassam, "Bullshit, Post-Truth, and Propaganda," in *Political Epistemology*, ed. Elizabeth Edenberg and Michael Hannon (Oxford: Oxford University Press, 2021), 49–63.

5. Uwe Peters and Nikolaj Nottelmann, "Weighing the Costs: The Epistemic Dilemma of No-Platforming," *Synthese* 199 (2021), DOI: 10.1007/s11229–021–03111-w.

6. Mill, *On Liberty*, 64.

7. Mill, *On Liberty*, 67.

8. See Mill, *On Liberty*, 67 and Peters and Nottelmann, "Weighing the Costs."

9. Michel Foucault, *The Government of Self and Others: Lectures at the Collège de France, 1982–1983*, trans. Graham Burchell (London: Palgrave/Macmillan, 2010), 182–84.

10. Richard Katz and Peter Mair, "Changing Models of Party Organization and Party Democracy: The Emergence of the Cartel Party," *Party Politics* 1, no. 1 (1995): 5–28; Jonathan Hopkin, *Anti-System Politics: The Crisis of Market Liberalism in Rich Democracies* (Oxford: Oxford University Press, 2020).

11. Foucault, *The Government of Self and Others*, 183.

12. Foucault, *The Hermeneutics of the Subject: Lectures at the Collège de France, 1981–1982*, trans. Graham Burchell (London: Palgrave/Macmillan, 2005), 135–36.

13. Foucault, *The Hermeneutics of the Subject*, 242.

14. Foucault, *The Hermeneutics of the Subject*, 349.

15. Foucault, *The Government of Self and Others*, 236.

16. Foucault, *The Government of Self and Others*, 236–37.

17. Plato, *Laws* 835b–c.

18. Plato, *Republic* 398–403.

19. Foucault, *The Government of Self and Others*, 211–14.

20. Plato, *Republic* 493a–b.

21. Foucault, *The Government of Self and Others*, 104–5.

22. Foucault, *The Hermeneutics of the Subject*, 372.

23. Geoffrey Bennington, *Scatter 1: The Politics of Politics in Foucault, Heidegger, and Derrida* (New York: Fordham University Press, 2016), 16–17.

24. Jacques Rancière, *Dis-agreement: Politics and Philosophy*, trans. Julie Roe (Minneapolis: University of Minnesota Press, 1999), 54.

25. Daniele Lorenzini, "Reason versus Power: Genealogy, Critique, and Epistemic Injustice," *The Monist* 105, no. 4 (2022): 541–57.

26. See, for example, Matthias Fritsch, "Deconstructive Aporias: Quasi-Transcendental and Normative," *Continental Philosophy Review* 44 (2011): 439–68; and Stella Gaon, "*Il la faut (la logique)*, Yes, Yes: Deconstruction's Critical Force," *Derrida Today* 11, no. 2 (2018): 196–210.

27. Sara Ahmed, *Willful Subjects* (Durham NC: Duke University Press, 2014), 30.

1. Martin Scherzinger, "The Political Economy of Streaming," in *The Cambridge Companion to Music in Digital Culture*, ed. Nicholas Cook, Monique M. Ingalls, and David Trippett (Cambridge: Cambridge University Press, 2019), 274–97.

2. Eric Drott, "Music as a Technology of Surveillance," *Journal of the Society for American Music* 12, no. 3 (1018): 233–67.

3. On portable listening devices, see Michael Bull's *Sounding out the City: Personal Stereos and the Management of Everyday Life* (Oxford: Berg, 2000) and *Sound Moves: iPod Culture and Urban Experience* (New York: Routledge, 2007).

4. Tia DeNora, "Music as a Technology of the Self," *Poetics* 27, no. 1 (1999): 31–56 and *Music and Everyday Life* (Cambridge: Cambridge University Press, 2000).

5. Naomi Waltham-Smith, *Music and Belonging between Revolution and Restoration* (New York: Oxford University Press, 2017).

6. Nick Seaver, "Algorithmic Recommendations and Synaptic Functions," *Limn* 2 (2012), https://limn.it/articles/algorithmic -recommendations-and-synaptic-functions.

7. K. E. Goldschmitt and Nick Seaver, "Shaping the Stream: Techniques and Troubles of Algorithmic Recommendation," in *The Cambridge Companion to Music in Digital Culture*, ed. Cook, Nicholas, Monique M. Ingalls, and David Trippett (Cambridge: Cambridge University Press, 2019), 70–71.

8. For a discussion of some of these apps, see Sumanth Gopinath and Jason Stanyek, "Technologies of the Musical Selfie," in *The Cambridge Companion to Music in Digital Culture*, 89–118.

9. Naomi Waltham-Smith, "The Sonic *Habitués* of the Strip: Listening in Las Vegas," *Sound Studies* 3, no. 2 (2018): 115–33.

10. Stéphan-Eloïse Gras, "L'écoute en ligne. Figures du sujet écoutant et mutations des espaces musicaux sur Internet" (PhD thesis, Paris 4, 2014).

11. Drott, "Music as a Technology of Surveillance," 245–46.

12. Luciana Parisi, "The Alien Subject of AI," *Subjectivity* 12 (2019): 27–48.

13. Gopinath and Stanyek, "Technologies of the Musical Selfie."

14. See the account in Pierre Dardot and Christian Laval, *The New Way of the World: On Neoliberal Society*, trans. Gregory Elliott (London: Verso, 2017).

15. Luc Boltanksi and Ève Chiapello, *The New Spirit of Capitalism*, trans. Gregory Elliott (London: Verso, 2005).

16. Olga Goriunova, "The Digital Subject: People as Data as Persons," *Theory, Culture and Society* 36, no. 6 (2019): 125–45.

17. David Wills, "Positive Feedback: Listening behind Hearing," in *Thresholds of Listening: Sound, Technics, Space*, ed. Sander van Maas (New York: Fordham University Press, 2015), 78.

18. Scott Wark, "The Subject of Circulation: On the Digital Subject's Technical Individuations," *Subjectivity* 12 (2019): 65–81.

19. Rei Terada, *Feeling in Theory: Emotion: After the "Death of the Subject"* (Cambridge MA: Harvard University Press, 2001).

20. Sianne Ngai, *Ugly Feelings* (Cambridge MA: Harvard University Press, 2005).

21. Robin James, "What is a Vibe? On Vibez, Moods, Feels, and Contemporary Finance Capitalism," *It's Her Factory Newsletter*, January 29, 2021, https://itsherfactory.substack.com/p/what-is-a-vibe; "Is a Vibe a Vibration? Plus Vibes as Lay Phenomenology," *It's Her Factory Newsletter*, January 21, 2022, https://itsherfactory.substack.com/p/is-a-vibe-a-vibration?utm_source=%2fsearch%2fvibe&utm_medium=reader2.

22. Terada, *Feeling in Theory*, 5.

23. Ngai, *Ugly Feelings*, 269–70.

IT'S ALL THE RAGE

1. Rei Terada, "Hegel's Racism for Radicals," *Radical Philosophy* 2, no. 5 (2019): 11–22.

2. Audre Lorde, "The Uses of Anger," *Women's Studies Quarterly* 9, no. 3 (1981): 7 (emphasis mine).

3. Eric Lonergan and Mark Blyth, *Angrynomics* (Newcastle: Agenda Publishing, 2000), 17–18.

4. John Stuart Mill, *On Liberty* (Cambridge: Cambridge University Press, 2011 [1859]), 98.

5. David Palumbo-Liu, *Speaking Out of Place: Getting Our Political Voices Back* (Chicago: Haymarket Books, 2021).

6. Police, Crime, Sentencing and Courts Act 2022 (UK).

7. "Noise-Related Provisions: Police, Crime, Sentencing and Courts Act 2022 Factsheet," updated August 2022, https://www.gov.uk /government/publications/police-crime-sentencing-and-courts -bill-2021-factsheets/police-crime-sentencing-and-courts-bill-2021 -noise-related-provisions-factsheet.

8. Lorde, "The Uses of Anger," 9.

9. Jacques Derrida, "Tympan," in *Margins of Philosophy,* trans. by Alan Bass (Chicago: University of Chicago Press), ix–xxix.

10. Lonergan and Blyth, *Angrynomics,* 54.

11. Lonergan and Blyth, *Angrynomics,* 9.

12. Sivamohan Valluvan, "The Clamour of Nationalism: Race and Nation in Twenty-First-Century Britain," (Manchester: Manchester University Press, 2019), 58–59.

13. Jean-François Lyotard, *The Differend: Phrases in Dispute,* trans. Georges Van Den Abbeele (Minneapolis: University of Minnesota Press, 1988). See also my "The Silences of Feeling," *Philosophy Today* 66, no. 2 (2022): 287–306.

14. bell hooks, *Killing Rage: Ending Racism* (New York: H. Holt, 1995), 12.

15. Sue J. Kim, *On Anger: Race, Cognition, Narrative* (Austin: University of Texas Press, 2013), 50.

16. hooks, *Killing Rage,* 20; cited in Kim, *On Anger,* 52.

17. Sonali Chakravarti, *Sing the Rage: Listening to Anger After Mass Violence* (Chicago: University of Chicago Press), 122 (citing Adam Smith).

18. Chakravarti, *Sing the Rage,* 169, 173.

19. Sam Binkley, "Black Rage and White Listening: On the Psychologization of Racial Emotionality," in *Race, Rage, and Resistance: Philosophy, Psychology, and the Perils of Individualism,* ed. David M. Goodman, Eric R. Severson, and Heather Macdonald (New York: Routledge, 2020), 93.

20. Theodore Reik, *Listening with the Third Ear: The Inner Experience of a Psychoanalyst* (New York: Grove Press, 1948), 116; cited in Binkley, "Black Rage, White Listening," 101.

21. Binkley, "Black Rage, White Listening," 104. On the racial contract, see Charles W. Mills, *The Racial Contract* (Ithaca: Cornell University Press, 1997).

22. Agnes Callard, "On Anger," *Boston Review*, Forum XIII (Winter 2020), https://bostonreview.net/forum/agnes-callard-philosophy-anger.

23. Martha C. Nussbaum, *Anger and Forgiveness: Resentment, Generosity, Justice* (New York: Oxford University Press, 2016), 3.

24. Myisha Cherry, "The Errors and Limitations of our 'Anger-Evaluating' Ways," in *The Moral Psychology of Anger*, ed. Cherry and Owen Flanagan (London: Rowan & Littlefield, 2018), 58.

25. Céline Leboeuf, "Anger as a Political Emotion: A Phenomenological Perspective," in *The Moral Psychology of Anger*, ed. Cherry and Flanagan, 21.

26. Amia Srinivasan, "The Aptness of Anger," *The Journal of Political Philosophy* 26, no. 2 (2018): 123–44.

27. Myisha Cherry, *The Case for Rage: Why Anger is Essential to Anti-Racist Struggle* (New York: Oxford University Press, 2021).

28. Brittney Cooper, *Eloquent Rage* (New York: St. Martin's Press, 2018), 170; cited in Cherry, *The Case for Rage*, 83.

29. Cherry, *The Case for Rage*, 24–25.

30. Cherry, "The Errors and Limitations," 64.

31. Leboeuf, "Anger."

32. Callard, "On Anger."

33. Miguel de Beistegui, *Thought under Threat: On Superstition, Spite, and Stupidity* (Chicago: University of Chicago Press, 2022).

34. Lorde, "The Use of Anger," 9.

35. Peter Szendy, *Of Stigmatology* (New York: Fordham University Press, 2018), 44–58, at 56.

36. Lauren Berlant, "Introduction: Compassion (and Withholding)," in *Compassion: The Culture and Politics of an Emotion*, ed. Lauren Berlant (New York: Routledge, 2004), 4.

37. Berlant, "Compassion," 8.

38. Srinivasan, "The Aptness of Anger," 132.

39. Lyotard, "Sensus Communis," trans. Marian Hobson and Geoff Bennington, *Paragraph* 11, no. 1 (1988): 12.

40. J. Hillis Miller, *Others* (Princeton NJ: Princeton University Press, 2001), 74–77.

LIES, BULLSHIT, AND SOPHISTRY

1. Thomas Docherty, "Academic and Other Freedoms," *Why Academic Freedom Matters: A Response to Current Challenges*, ed. Cheryl Hudson and Joanna Williams (London: Civitas, 2016), 99.

2. Kharlamov v. Russia, App. No. 27447/07 (ECtHR October 8, 2015), 29; Sorguç v. Turkey, App. No 17089/03 (ECtHR June 23, 2009), 31–26, at 35, repeating the formulation in UNESCO Recommendation (1997), section VI.A. §27; See also Rubins v. Latvia, App. No. 79040/12, (ECtHR January 13, 2015).

3. *Kharlamov*, 32.

4. Palomo Sánchez and Others v. Spain, App. Nos. 28955/06, 28957/06, 28959/06 and 28964/06 (ECtHR September 12, 2011), 76.

5. The formulation first appeared in Handyside v. United Kingdom [1976] 1 EHRR 737, 49 and has since been much cited in Article 10 cases at the ECtHR and in domestic courts.

6. *Palomo Sánchez*, 15.

7. Evyn Lê Espiritu, Jasbir K. Puar, and Steven Salaita, "Civility, Academic Freedom, and the Project of Decolonization: A Conversation with Steven Salaita," *Qui Parle: Critical Humanities and Social Sciences* 24, no. 1 (2015), 63–88.

8. Arianne Shahvisi, "On the Social Epistemology of Academic Freedom," in *Civility, Free Speech, and Academic Freedom in Higher Education: Faculty on the Margins*, ed. Reshmi Dutt-Ballerstadt and Kakali Bhattacharya (New York: Routledge, 2021), 59–71

9. Teresa M. Bejan, *Mere Civility: Disagreement and the Limits of Toleration* (Cambridge MA: Harvard University Press, 2017).

10. Shahvisi, "On the Social Epistemology of Academic Freedom," 67.

11. Jacques Derrida, "Mochlos, or The Conflict of the Faculties," trans. Jan Plug, in *Eyes of the University: Right to Philosophy 2* (Stanford CA: Stanford University Press, 2004), 83–112.

12. Mustafa Erdoğan and others v. Turkey [2014] ECHR 673 (nos. 346/04 and 39779/04), §6; see also the joint concurring opinion, §§8–10. On the meaning of "field of expertise," see the then minister of state for universities' comments in the Commons Public Bill Committee,

September 15, 2021, https://publications.parliament.uk/pa/bills
/cbill/58-02/0012/amend/pbc012_HigherEducationBill_1st_12th
_Compilation_22_09_2021.pdf.

13. Aksu v. Turkey, App. Nos. 4149/04 and 41029/04 (ECtHR March 15, 2012).

14. Michel Foucault, "Orders of Discourse," trans. Rupert Swyer, *Social Science Information* 10, no. 2 (1971): 16.

15. Foucault, "Orders of Discourse," 15.

16. Robert Post, "The Classic First Amendment Tradition Under Stress: Freedom of Speech and the University," in *The Free Speech Century*, ed. Lee C. Bollinger and Geoffrey R. Stone (Oxford: Oxford University Press, 2018), 115–16.

17. Joan Wallach Scott, *Knowledge, Power, and Academic Freedom* (New York: Columbia University Press, 2019), 52.

18. Bonn Declaration on Freedom of Scientific Research, adopted by the European Research Area on October 20, 2020, https://www.bmbf
.de/bmbf/shareddocs/downloads/files/_drp-efr-bonner_erklaerung
_en_with-signatures_maerz_2021.pdf?_blob=publicationFile&v=1.

19. Talia Mae Bettcher, "'When Tables Speak': On the Existence of Trans Philosophy," *Daily Nous*, May 30, 2018, https://dailynous.com
/2018/05/30/tables-speak-existence-trans-philosophy-guest-talia
-mae-bettcher/.

20. Geoffrey Bennington, *Scatter 2* (New York: Fordham University Press, 2020), 9.

21. Miguel de Beistegui, *Thought under Threat: On Superstition, Spite, and Stupidity* (Chicago: University of Chicago Press, 2022).

22. Uwe Peters and Nikolaj Nottelmann, "Weighing the Costs: The Epistemic Dilemma of No-Platforming," *Synthese* 199 (2021), DOI: 10.1007/s11229-021-03111-w.

23. Quassim Cassam, *Vices of the Mind: From the Intellectual to the Political* (Oxford: Oxford University Press, 2019), 35.

24. Cassam, *Vices*, 115.

25. Cassam, *Vices*, 113.

26. David Palumbo-Liu, "Why we have free speech on university campuses, and why I will never take a call from the Stanford Review again," *The Stanford Daily*, January 18, 2018, https://www
.stanforddaily.com/2018/01/18/why-we-have-free-speech-on

-university-campuses-and-why-i-will-never-take-a-call-from-the
-stanford-review-again.

27. Jacques Derrida, "Otobiographies," trans. Avital Ronell, in *The Ear of the Other: Otobiography, Transference, Translation*, ed. Christie McDonald (New York: Schocken Books, 1985), 4.

28. On "excluding the excluders," see Michael Bérubé and Jennifer Ruth, *It's Not Free Speech: Race, Democracy, and the Future of Academic Freedom* (Baltimore MD: John Hopkins University Press, 2022), 197.

29. John Stuart Mill, *On Liberty* (Cambridge: Cambridge University Press, 2011), 96.

30. De Beistegui, *Thought under Threat*, 35.

31. Gilles Deleuze, *Nietzsche and Philosophy*, trans. Hugh Tomlinson (New York: Columbia University Press, 1983), 105.

32. Jacques Derrida, *The Beast and the Sovereign, Volume 1*, trans. Geoffrey Bennington (Chicago: Chicago University Press, 2009), 148.

33. Julia Schleck, *Dirty Knowledge: Academic Freedom in the Age of Neoliberalism* (Lincoln: University of Nebraska Press, 2022).

UNHEARD

1. Naomi Waltham-Smith, "Who Gets a Hearing? Academic Freedom and Critique in Derrida's Reading of Kant," *Paragraph* 46, no. 3 (2023): 317–336.

2. Jacques Derrida, *Rogues: Two Essays on Reason*, trans. Pascale-Anne Bault and Michael Naas (Stanford CA: Stanford University Press, 2005), 142.

3. Saidiya Hartman, *Scenes of Subjection: Terror, Slavery, and Self-Making in Nineteenth-Century America* (Oxford: Oxford University Press, 1997), 11.

4. Hartman, *Scenes of Subjection*, 11–12.

5. Hartman, "Venus in Two Acts," *Small Axe* 12, no. 2 (2008): 11.

6. Hartman, "Venus," 12.

7. Hartman, "Venus," 2–3.

8. Fred Moten, "On Radical Indistinctness and Thought Flavor à la Derrida," interview with Adam Fitzgerald, *Literary Hub*, August 6, 2015, https://lithub.com/an-interview-with-fred-moten-pt-ii/.

9. W. E. B. Du Bois, *Black Reconstruction in America, 1860–1880* (New York: The Free Press, 1998 [1935]); Angela Davis, *Abolition Democracy:*

Beyond Prison, Torture, and Empire (New York: Seven Stories Press, 2005).

10. Jacques Derrida, "Le silence," unpublished seminar, Archive-Derrida, IMEC, 219DRR/218/3, 1959–60; "Entretien sur le silence, la responsabilité, la justice," unpublished interview with Alexander García Düttmann, Archive-Derrida, IMEC, 219DRR/257/1, 1988–89.

11. Theo Jung, "*Le silence du peuple*: The Rhetoric of Silence during the French Revolution," *French History* 31, no. 4, December (2017): 440–69.

12. Jung, "*Le silence du peuple*," 454.

13. Jeremy Bentham, "Traité des sophismes politiques," in *Tactique des assemblées législatives, suivi d'un traité des sophismes politiques*, ed. Étienne Dumont (Geneva and Paris, 1816), 88; cited in Jung, "*Le silence du peuple*," 458.

14. Kristie Dotson, "A Cautionary Tale: On Limiting Epistemic Oppression," *Frontiers* 33, no. 1 (2012): 24–47.

15. Miranda Fricker, *Epistemic Injustice: Power and the Ethics of Knowing* (Oxford: Oxford University Press, 2007).

16. Fricker, *Epistemic Injustice*, 43.

17. Edward Craig, *Knowledge and the State of Nature: An Essay in Conceptual Synthesis* (Oxford: Clarendon Press, 1990); Bernard Williams, *Truth and Truthfulness: An Essay in Genealogy* (Princeton NJ: Princeton University Press, 2002).

18. Fricker, *Epistemic Injustice*, 80.

19. Fricker, *Epistemic Injustice*, 74.

20. Matthieu Queloz, *The Practical Origins of Ideas: Genealogy as Conceptual-Reverse Engineering* (Oxford: Oxford University Press, 2021), 193–94. For a thorough critique of this move that will be discussed in greater detail in due course, see Daniele Lorenzini, "Reason Versus Power: Genealogy, Critique, and Epistemic Injustice," *The Monist* 105 (2022): 541–57.

21. Fricker, "Evolving Concepts of Epistemic Injustice," in *The Routledge Handbook of Epistemic Injustice*, ed. Ian Kidd, José Medina, and Gaile Pohlhaus (London: Routledge, 2017), 56.

22. Fricker, *Epistemic Injustice*, 3.

23. Fricker, "Evolving Concepts of Epistemic Injustice," 56.

24. Daniele Lorenzini, *The Force of Truth: Critique, Genealogy, and Truth-Telling in Michel Foucault* (Chicago: Chicago University Press, 2023), 2.

25. Lorenzini, "Reason Versus Power," 547–51.

26. Lorenzini, *The Force of Truth*, 2.

27. Ishani Maitra, "The Nature of Epistemic Injustice," *Philosophical Books* 51, no. 4 (2010): 197–211; Rebecca Mason, "Two Kinds of Unknowing," *Hypatia* 26, no. 2 (2011): 294–307.

28. Dotson, "A Cautionary Tale," 31.

29. Fricker, *Epistemic Injustice*, 74.

30. Lorenzini, "Reason Versus Power," 551.

31. José Medina, "Toward a Foucaultian Epistemology of Resistance: Counter-Memory, Epistemic Friction, and *Guerrilla* Pluralism," *Foucault Studies* 12 (2011): 9–35.

32. Dotson, "A Cautionary Tale," 35.

33. Françoise Vergès, "Fire, Anger and Humiliation in the Museum," in *Kader Attia: The Museum of Emotion*, exhibition catalog (London: Hayward Gallery Publishing, 2019), 86–87.

EARS FOR A MINOR MUSIC

1. Saidiya Hartman, "The End of White Supremacy, An American Romance," in *BOMB Magazine*, June 5, 2020, https://bombmagazine.org/articles/the-end-of-white-supremacy-an-american-romance.

2. W. E. B. Du Bois, "The Comet," in *Darkwater: Voices from within the Veil* (New York: Harcourt, Brace and Howe, 1920), 269.

3. Jacques Derrida, "Le silence," unpublished seminar, Archive-Derrida, IMEC, 219DRR/218/3, 1959–60.

4. Martin Heidegger, *Heraclitus: The Inception of Occidental Thinking Logic: Heraclitus's Doctrine of the Logos*, trans. Julia Goesser Assaiante and S. Montgomery Ewegen (London: Bloomsbury, 2018), 187ff.

5. Heidegger, *Heraclitus*, 188.

6. Heidegger, *Heraclitus*, 189.

7. Sylvia Wynter, "Unsettling the Coloniality of Being/Power/Truth/Freedom: Towards the Human, After Man, Its Overrepresentation—An Argument," *CR: The New Centennial Review* 3, no. 3 (2003): 257–337.

8. Rei Terada, "Hegel's Racism for Radicals," *Radical Philosophy* 2, no. 5 (2019): 11–22.

9. On Derrida's observation that the human is uniquely capable of being quiet, rather than simply mute, see Jacques Derrida, "Entretien sur le silence, la responsabilité, la justice," unpublished interview with Alexander García Düttmann, Archive-Derrida, IMEC, 219DRR/257/1, 1988–89.

10. Kathryn Yusoff, *A Billion Black Anthropocenes or None* (Minneapolis: University of Minnesota Press, 2019), 50.

11. Françoise Vergès, "Capitalocene, Waste, Race, and Gender," *e-flux* 100 (May 2019), https://www.e-flux.com/journal/100/269165/capitalocene-waste-race-and-gender.

12. Dipesh Chakrabarty, "Anthropocene Time," *History and Theory* 57, no. 1 (2018): 5–32.

13. Saidiya Hartman, "The End of White Supremacy, An American Romance," in *BOMB Magazine*, June 5, 2020, https://bombmagazine.org/articles/the-end-of-white-supremacy-an-american-romance.

14. Philippe Lynes, "Extinction and Thalassal Regression," *Oxford Literary Review* 41, no. 1 (2019): 108.

15. Naomi Waltham-Smith, "Turning Ears; Or Ec(h)otechnics," *Diacritics* 47, no. 4 (2019) :110–29.

16. David Wills, *Killing Times: The Temporal Technology of the Death Penalty* (New York: Fordham University Press, 2019), 88.

17. David Wills, *Dorsality: Thinking Back through Technology and Politics* (Minneapolis: University of Minnesota Press, 2008); "Positive Feedback: Listening Behind Hearing," in *Thresholds of Listening: Sound, Technics, Space*, ed. Sander van Maas (New York: Fordham University Press, 2015), 70–88.

18. David Wills, *Inanimation: Theories of Inorganic Life* (Minneapolis: University of Minnesota Press, 2016).

19. David Palumbo-Liu, *Speaking Out of Place: Getting Our Political Voices Back* (Chicago: Haymarket Books, 2021), 2.

20. Alexis Pauline Gumbs, *Undrowned: Black Feminist Lessons from Marine Mammals* (Chico CA: AK Press, 2020), 15.

21. Peter Szendy, "The Auditory Re-Turn (The Point of Listening)," in *Thresholds of Listening: Sound, Technics, Space*, ed. Sander vas Maas (New York: Fordham University Press, 2015), 27–29.

22. Jacques Derrida, *The Beast and the Sovereign, Volume 1*, trans. Geoffrey Bennington (Chicago: Chicago University Press, 2009), 74.

23. Derrida, *The Beast and the Sovereign I*, 15.

24. Dylan Robinson, *Hungry Listening: Resonant Theory for Indigenous Sound Studies* (Minneapolis: University of Minnesota Press, 2020).

25. "About Provocations Books," https://www.provocationsbooks.com/about.

26. Lauren Berlant, "Genre Flailing," *Capacious: Journal for Emerging Affect Inquiry* 1, no. 2 (2018): 156–62. See also "Big Man," January 19, 2017, https://socialtextjournal.org/big-man.

27. Berlant, "Genre Flailing," 157.

28. Berlant, "Genre Flailing," 160.

29. Françoise Vergès, "A Leap of Imagination," in *Slow Spatial Reader: Chronicles of Radical Affection*, ed. Carolyn F. Strauss (Amsterdam: Valiz, 2021), 219–29.

30. Vergès, "A Leap of Imagination," 229.

31. Françoise Vergès, "Politics of Marooning and Radical Disobedience," *e-flux* 105 (December 2019), https://www.e-flux.com/journal/105/305244/politics-of-marooning-and-radical-disobedience.

32. Berlant, "Genre Flailing," 157 (my substitution of "hearing" for "viewing").

33. Anne Dufourmantelle, *In Defence of Secrets*, trans. Lindsay Turner (New York: Fordham University Press, 2021), 104.

34. Vergès, "Politics of Marooning."

35. Anne Dufourmantelle, *Power of Gentleness: Meditations on the Risk of Living*, trans. Katherine Payne and Vincent Sallé (New York: Fordham University Press, 2018), 110–12.

To order or obtain more information on these or other University of Nebraska Press titles, visit nebraskapress.unl.edu.